St. George Ontario Book 2 and Bethel, Oakland and Scotland in Colour Photos, Saving Our History One Photo at a Time

Photography
by Barbara Raué
2017

Series Name:
Cruising Ontario

Book 181: St. George Book 2 and Bethel Road, Oakland and Scotland

Cover photo: 27 Talbot Street, Scotland, Page 55

Series Name: Cruising Ontario
Saving Our History One Photo at a Time
in colour photos

Books Available in Alphabetical Order:
Aberfoyle, Acton, Alton, Amherstburg, Ancaster, Arthur, Aylmer, Ayr, Bloomingdale, Brantford, Burlington, Caledon, Caledonia, Cambridge, Clifford, Conestogo, Delhi, Dorchester to Aylmer, Drayton, Drumbo, Dundas, Eden Mills, Elmira, Elora, Essex, Fergus, Guelph, Hagersville, Hamilton, Hanover, Harriston, Hespeler, Jarvis, Kingston, Kingsville, Kitchener, Linwood, Listowel, London, Lucknow, Mono, Mount Forest, Neustadt, New Hamburg, Niagara-on-the-Lake, Oakville, Orangeville, Orillia, Owen Sound, Palmerston, Peterborough, Petrolia, Port Elgin, Preston, Rockwood, Sarnia, Seaforth, Sheffield, Shelburne, Simcoe, Southampton, St. Jacobs, St. Marys, St. Thomas, Stoney Creek, Stratford, Thamesford, Tillsonburg, Waterdown, Waterford, Waterloo, Welland, Wellesley, Windsor, Wingham, Woodstock

Book 146-149: Ottawa
Book 156: Morrisburg
Book 157: Brockville
Book 158: Merrickville
Book 159: Smiths Falls
Book 160: Portland, Newboro
Book 161: Westport & Area
Book 162: Perth
Book 163-166: Belleville
Book 167-168: Port Colborne
Book 169: Erin in Colour
Book 170: Goderich in Colour
Book 171: Sault Ste. Marie
Book 172: Lake Superior
Book 173-176: Thunder Bay
Book 177-179: Paris
Book 180-181: St. George
Book 182-183: Burford
Book 184: Mt Pleasant, Onondaga, Newport

Other Books by Barbara Raue

Coins of Gold

Arrows, Indians and Love

The Life and Times of Barbara
Volume 1: Inventions That Have Enhanced My Life
Volume 2: Entertainment That I Have Enjoyed
Volume 3: East Coast Trips
Volume 4: Olympics Have Always Intrigued Me
Volume 5: Wonders of the World
Volume 6: Caribbean Cruises We Have Enjoyed
Volume 7: Animals
Volume 8: Storms and Other Major Disasters in My Lifetime
Volume 9: Wars, Terrorist Attacks and Major Disasters

The Cromwell Family Book

Laura Secord Discovered

Daddy Where Are You?

Montana Series
Book 1: Montana Dream
Book 2: Life on the Montana Frontier
Book 3: Montana to Boston and Back
Book 4: Montana Sons Go to War
Book 5: Montana Sons Return From War

Visit Barbara's website to view all of her books
http://barbararaue.ca

Table of Contents

St. George
- Lorimer Street — Page 7
- King William Street — Page 10
- Reid Street — Page 16
- St. George Road — Page 20
- McLean School Road — Page 21
- Branchton Road — Page 23
- Glen Morris Road East — Page 24
- 359 Regional Road 35 — Page 29

Bethel Road — Page 30

Township of Oakland
- Oakland — Page 43
- Scotland — Page 51

Architectural Terms — Page 66

Building Styles — Page 69

The County of Brant is located at the mid-point of the Grand River as it flows south from Luther Marsh to Lake Erie.

In 1852 the City of Brantford, the Village of Paris, and the Townships of Brantford, Oakland, Onondaga, South Dumfries, and Burford became Brant County.

Two hundred years ago, Obed Wilson ventured forth seeking an area in Upper Canada in which to settle. He discovered a place with fertile land, sparkling water and natural beauty which enticed him to stay and build a log cabin. Eventually the vision grew into the Village of St. George.

St. George, located to the north of the City of Brantford, is in the Township of South Dumfries. It was founded in 1814. John and Peter Bauslaugh were early settlers in St. George, and the early name of the village was "Bauslaugh Mills" in honour of John Bauslaugh who owned a sawmill near Highway 99. Main Street began to develop in the 1820s when Henry Moe began selling fish and dry goods from the first log building. By 1832, the village had three churches and several businesses. Today Main Street continues to thrive with many of the original buildings from the 1800s attracting people to the antique shops, cafes and restaurants.

The community around Bethel Road with Rest Acres Road to the east and the Bishopsgate Road to the west was settled in the 1830s. The major industry in this area was farming. Some of its first settlers were the Gurneys, McAllisters (wagon maker), Aulsebrooks, Lovetts and Major Arnold Burrowes whose 1,000 acre estate was known as Strathmore. On his estate Major Burrowes constructed a mill dam, stock pens, hop mill, a distillery, a grist mill and a plaster mill.

The Township of Oakland includes the towns of Scotland and Oakland. It has a rich history.

Scotland is located on the Burford/Oakland township line. The village was surveyed and laid out by Eliakim Malcolm. The first hotel opened in 1830, the first story in 1837 and the first post office in 1855. Malcolm's Creek had enough waterpower to sustain several industries such as a woollen mill, gristmill, tannery and foundry. Other early industries were a cooperage, a wagon and carriage works, carriage and buggy works and a starch factory. Two doctors and a lawyer practiced in Scotland in the mid-1800s.

Dr. Charles Duncombe (1791-1867), a prominent doctor and politician, was leader of the militant reform movement in the London district at the time of the Rebellion of 1837. He rallied the local Patriots at the settlement of Scotland, planning to move against Brantford and Hamilton and join forces with William Lyon Mackenzie King. On December 13, 1837, word was received of King's defeat at Montgomery's Tavern and of Colonel Allan MacNab's approach with a strong Loyalist force. Disheartened, Duncombe's followers dispersed during the night and he fled to the United States.

The Village of Oakland is located three kilometers east of Scotland on the Oakland Road. Oakland was named for a ridge of oak trees that ran through it. In 1850, the first municipal office was at the Oakland Post Office. A town hall was built in 1854 and Council met there until the early 1900s. Oakland had a grist mill in 1806, saw mill in 1807, a cheese factory, cider mill, three general stores, a shoemaker, harness maker, and a hotel.

Oakland is the site of the Battle of Malcolm Mills which was the last land battle of the War of 1812 on Canadian soil against an official foreign power. The battle took place at the stream that runs through Lion's Park. In October 1814, an invading American force of about seven hundred men under Brigadier-General Duncan McArthur advanced rapidly up the Thames Valley. He intended to devastate the Grand River settlements and the region around the head of Lake Ontario, which supplied British forces on the Niagara Frontier. McArthur reached the Grand, and after an unsuccessful attempt to force a crossing, attacked a body of about one hundred and fifty militia at Malcom's Mills (Oakland) on November 6th. Canadian forces put up a spirited resistance but were overwhelmed.

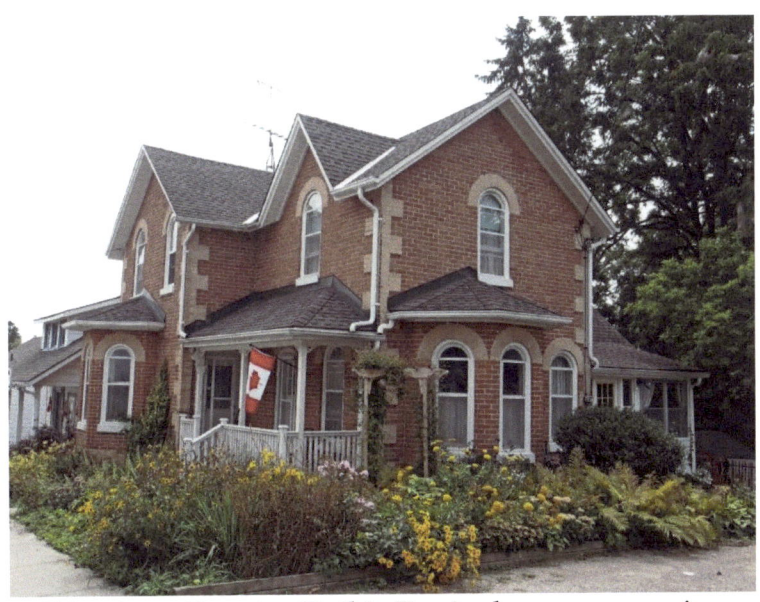

5 Lorimer Street – Gothic Revival – corner quoins

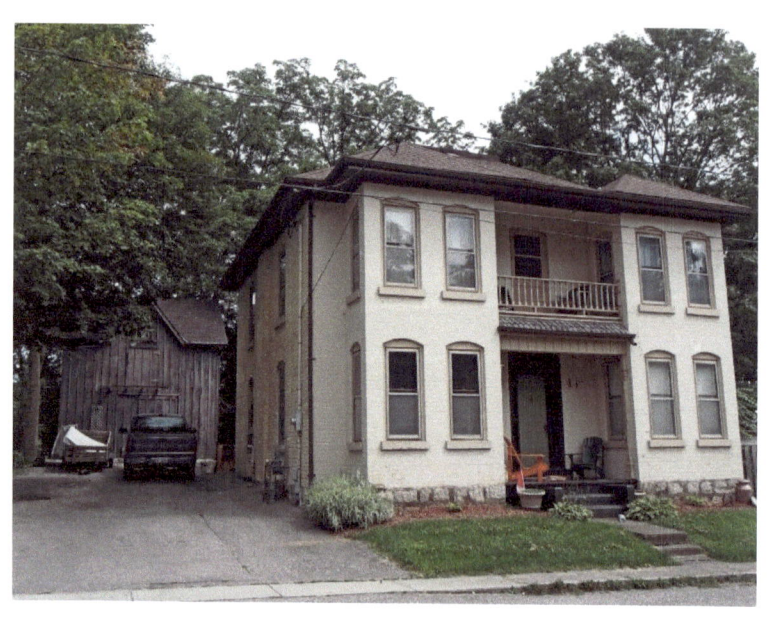

4 Lorimer Street – hipped roof

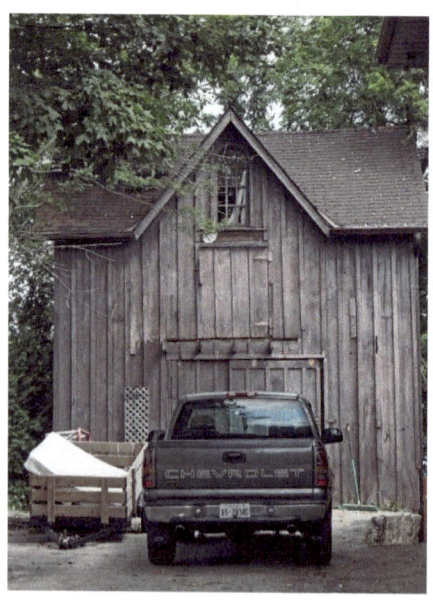

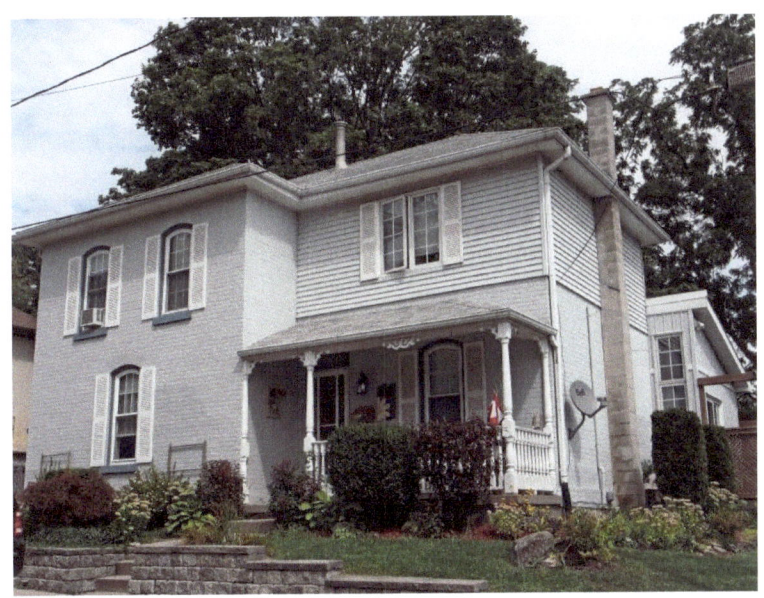

6 Lorimer Street

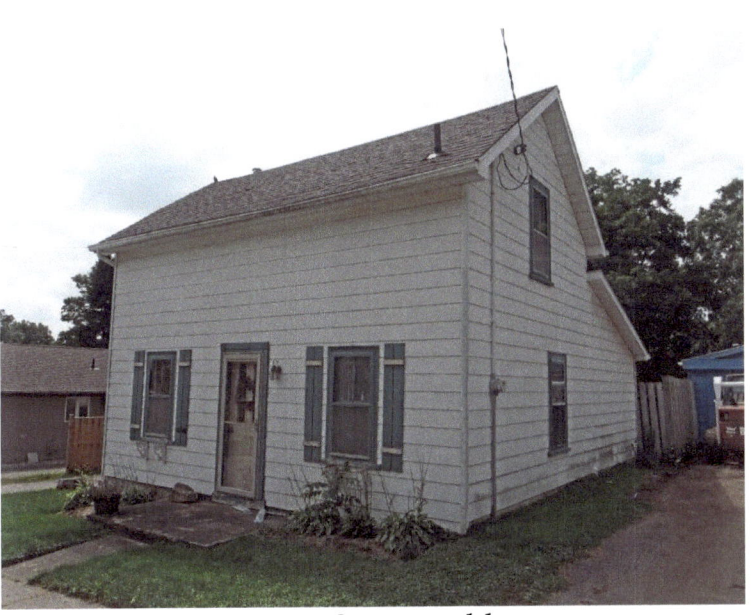

Lorimer Street - saltbox

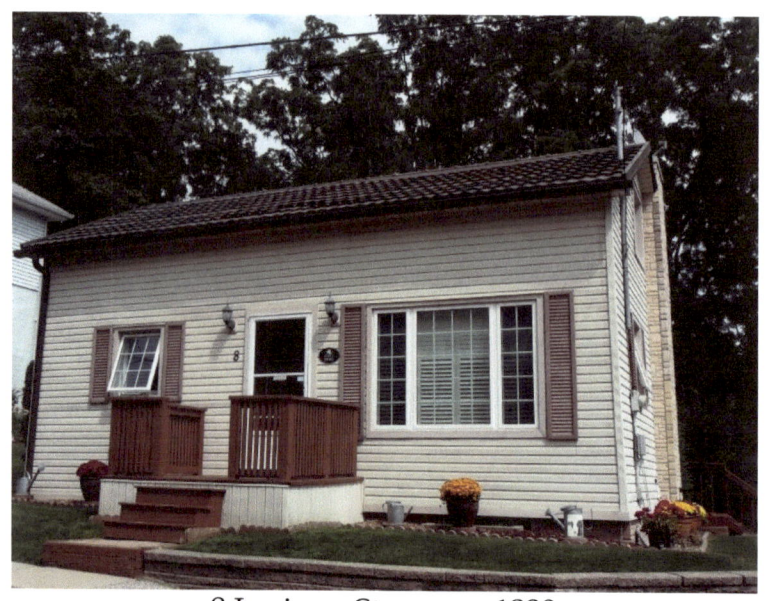
8 Lorimer Street – c. 1880

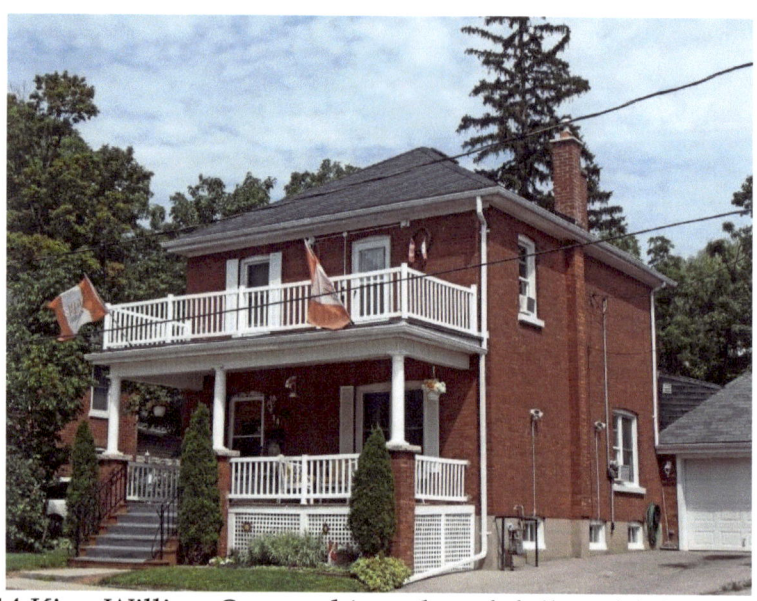
14 King William Street – hipped roof, full-width balcony above veranda

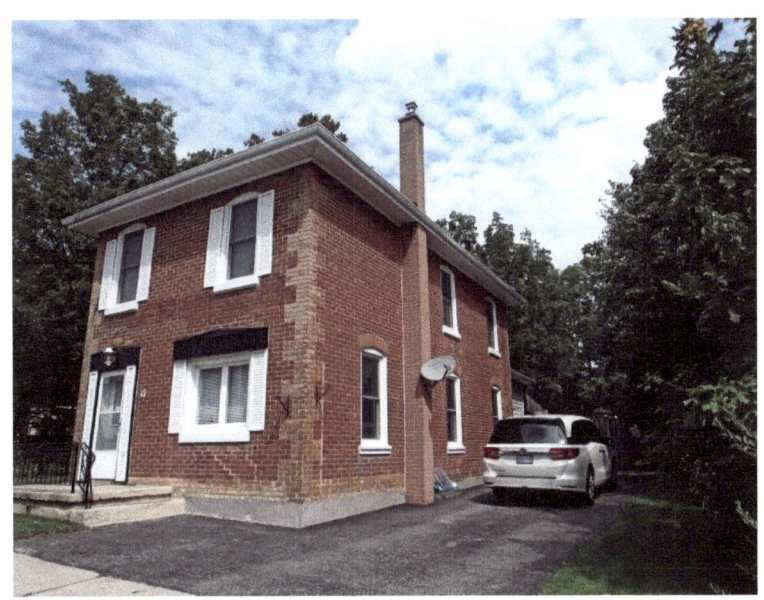

12 King William Street – corner quoins

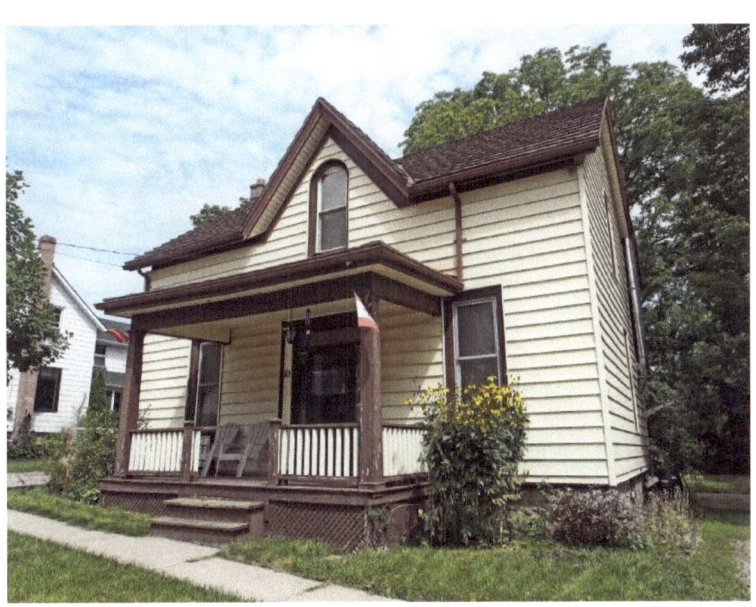

10 King William Street – Ontario Cottage

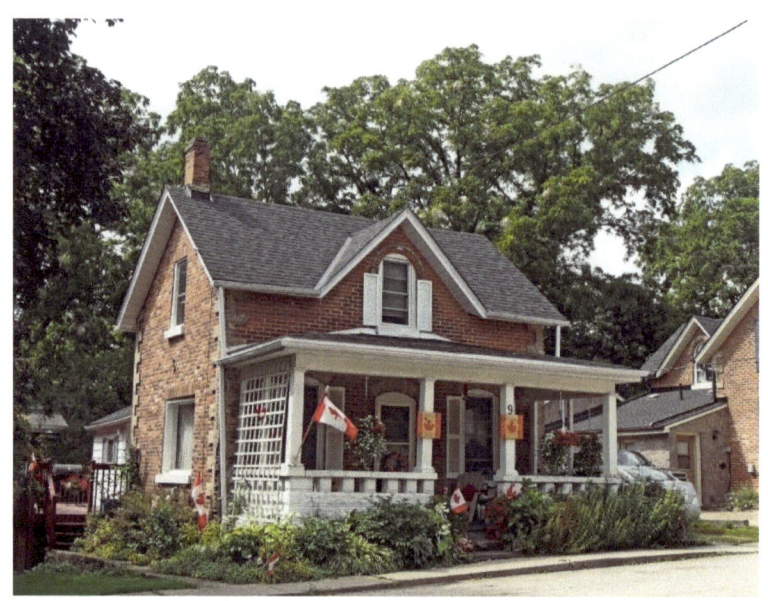
9 King William Street – Gothic, corner quoins

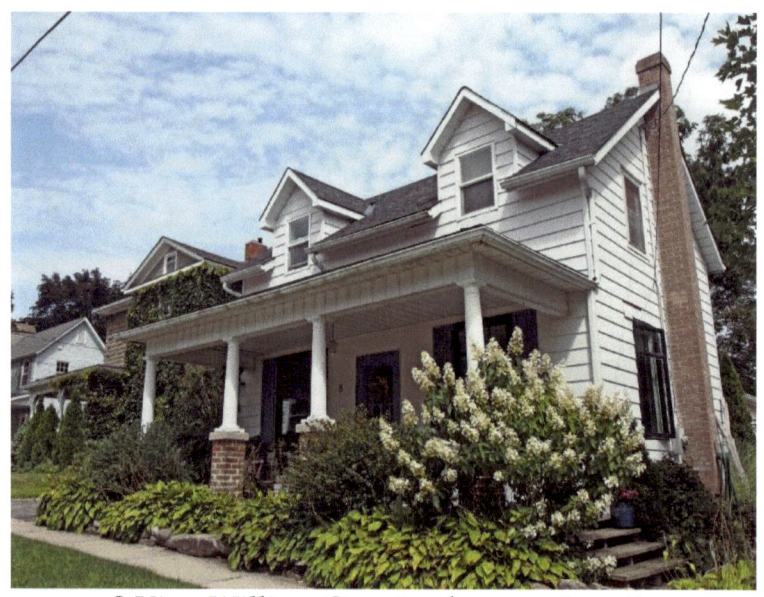
8 King William Street – dormers in attic

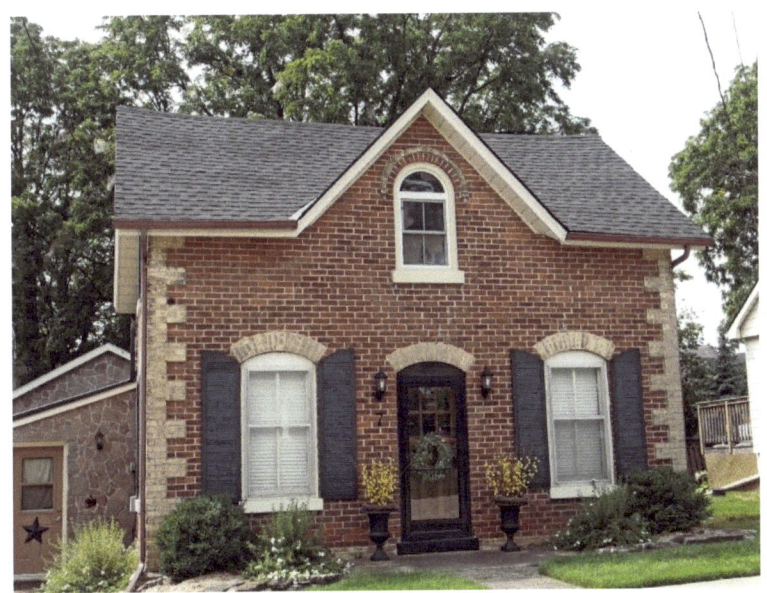

7 King William Street – Gothic, corner quoins, voussoirs

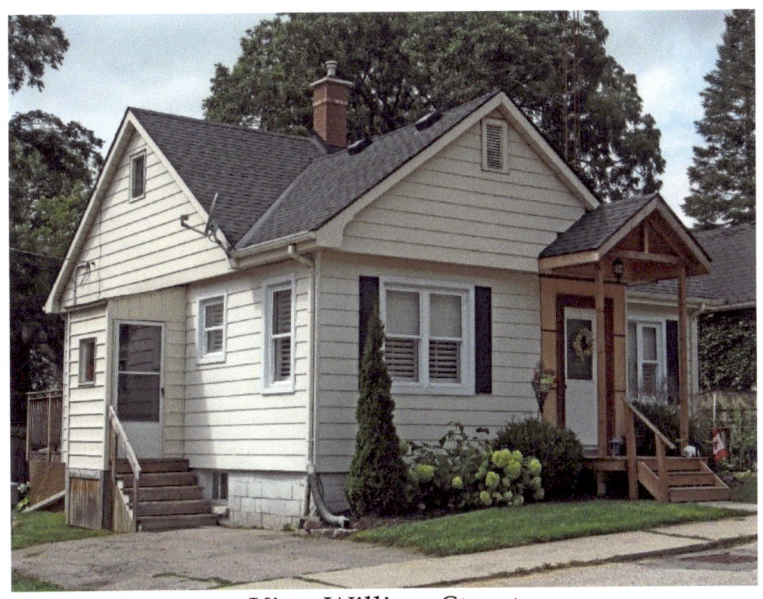

King William Street

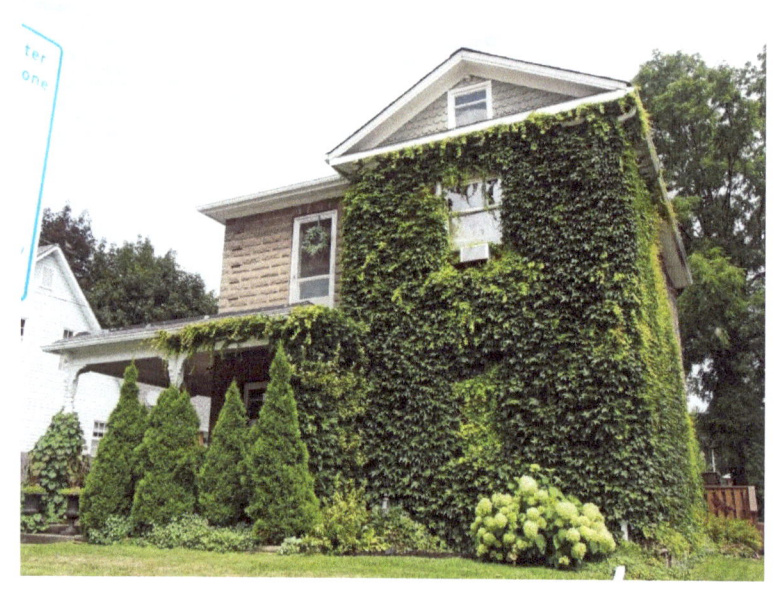

6 King William Street – vines taking over

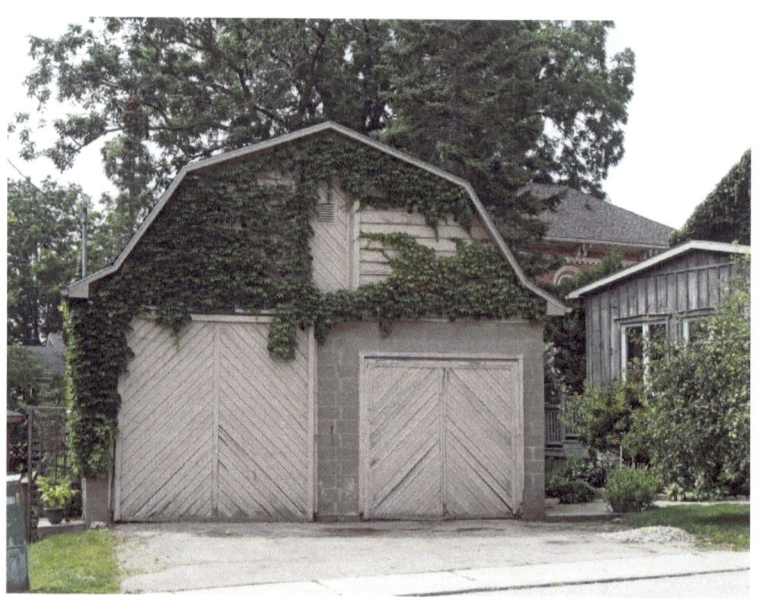

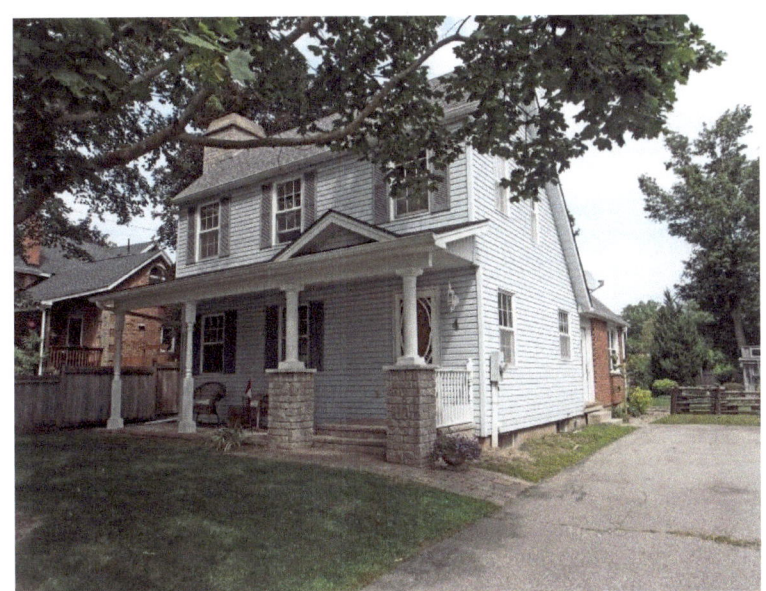

4 King William Street – pediment

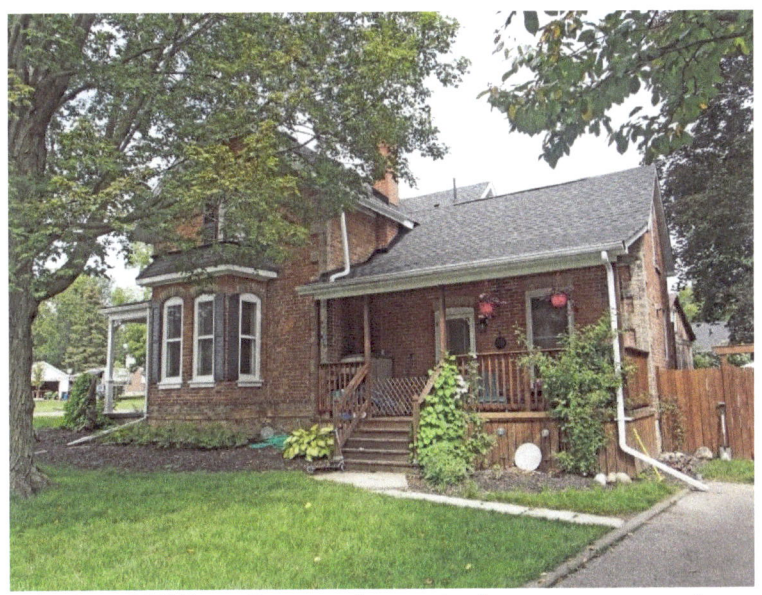

2 King William Street – bay window, corner quoins

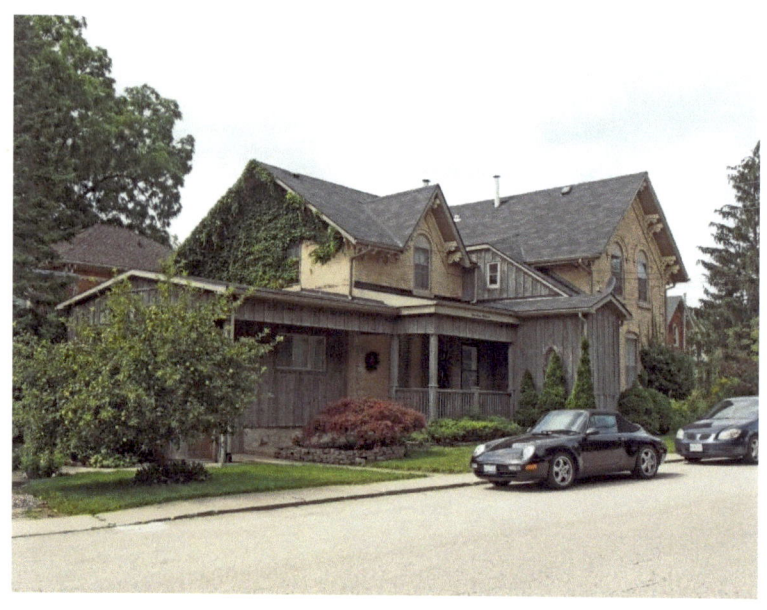

1 King William Street – Gothic Revival, paired cornice brackets

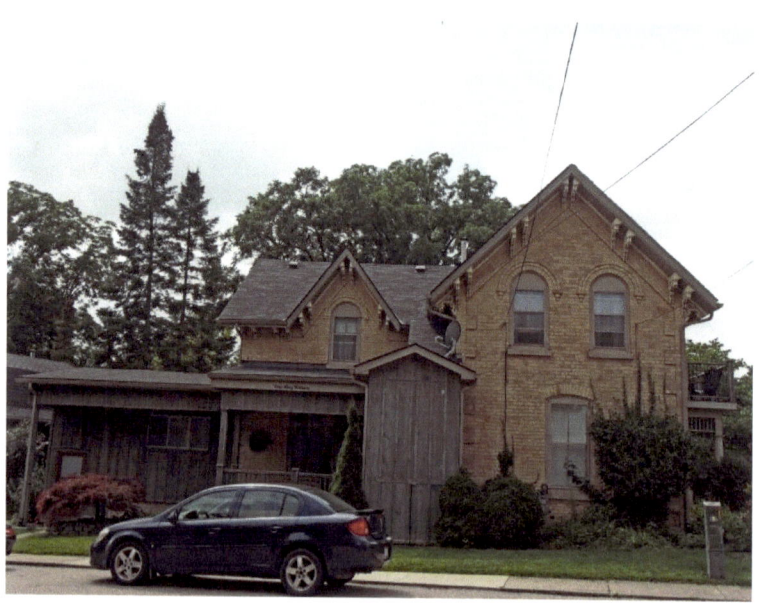

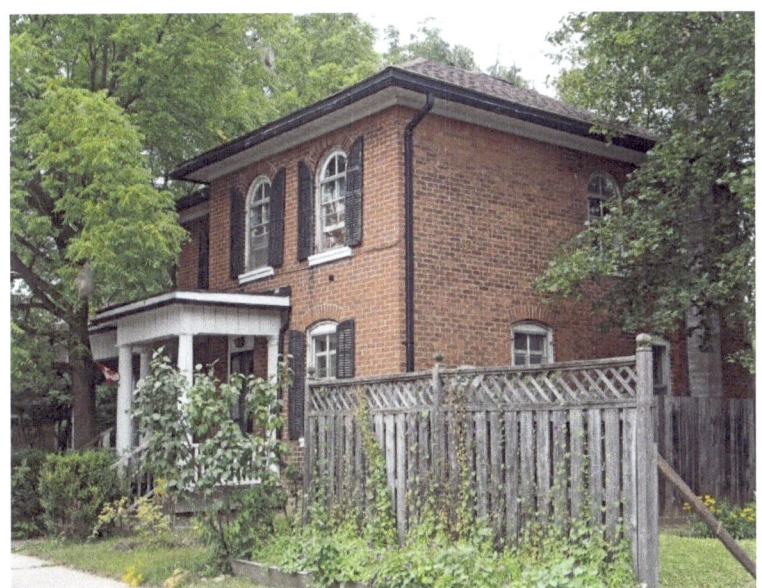

2 Reid Street – hipped roof, half-round windows with shutters

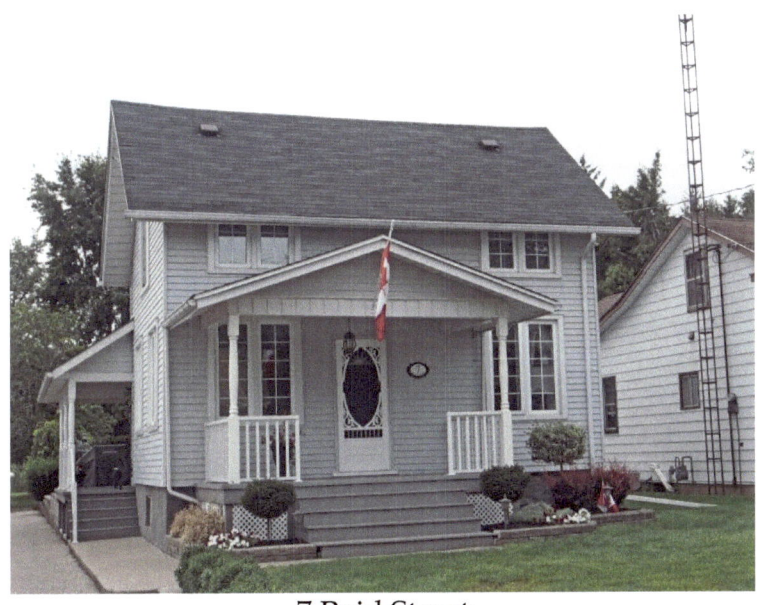

7 Reid Street

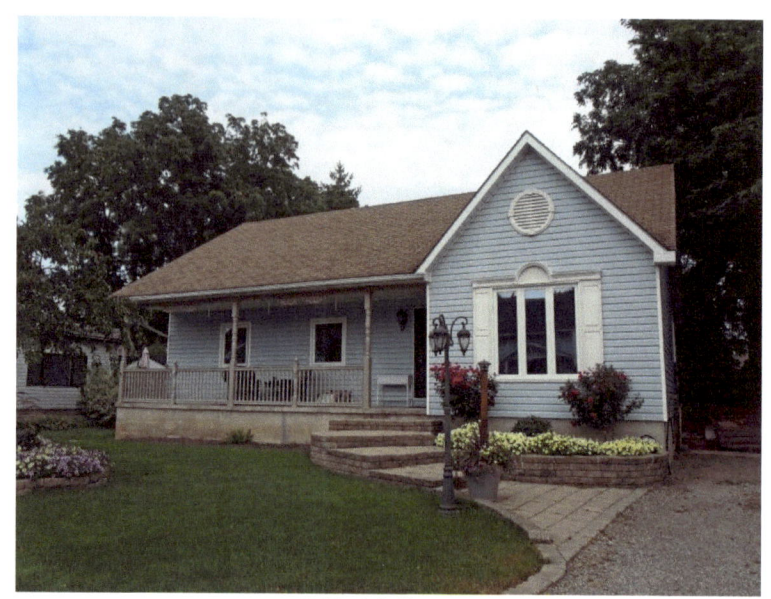

8 Reid Street

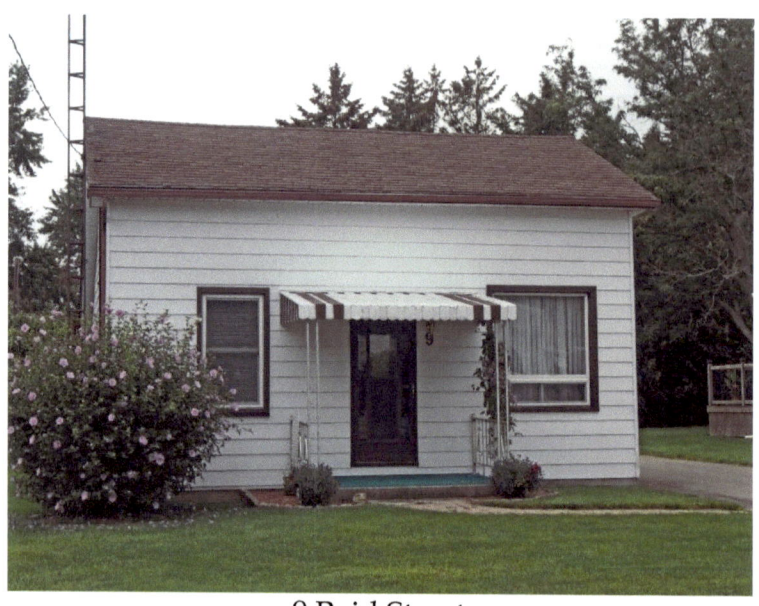

9 Reid Street

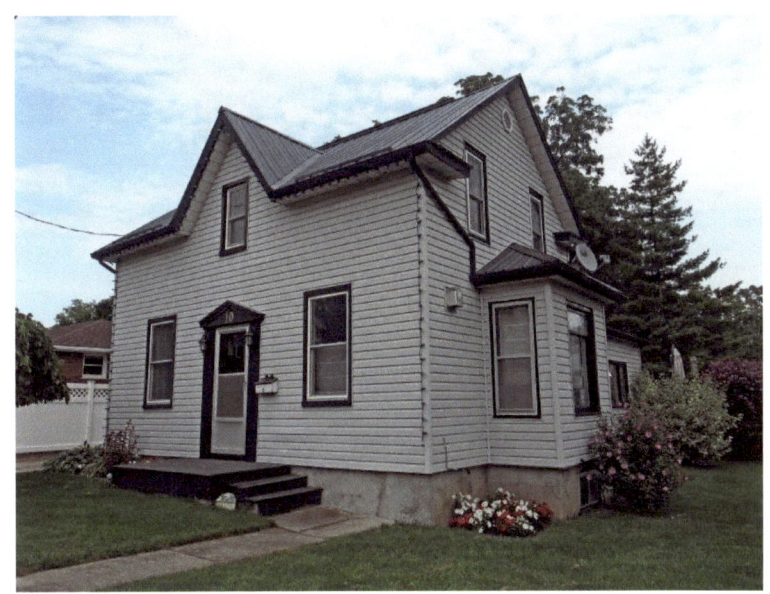

10 Reid Street - Gothic

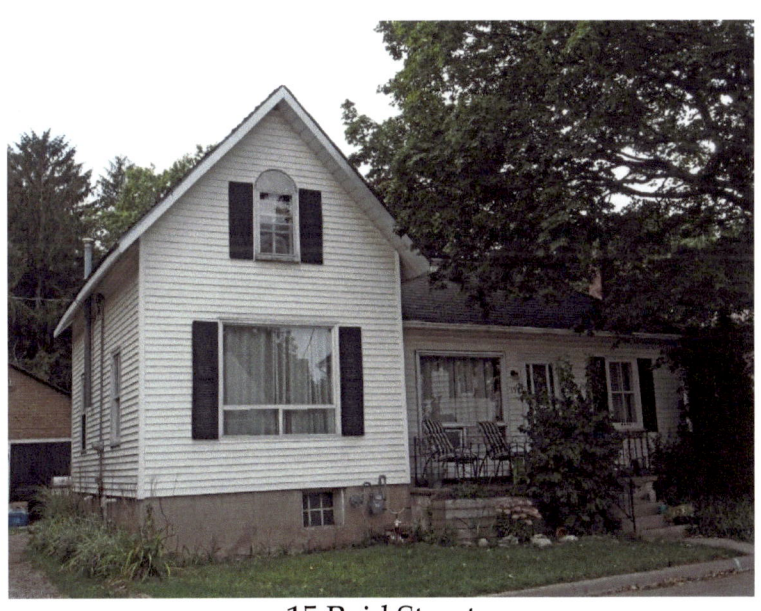

15 Reid Street

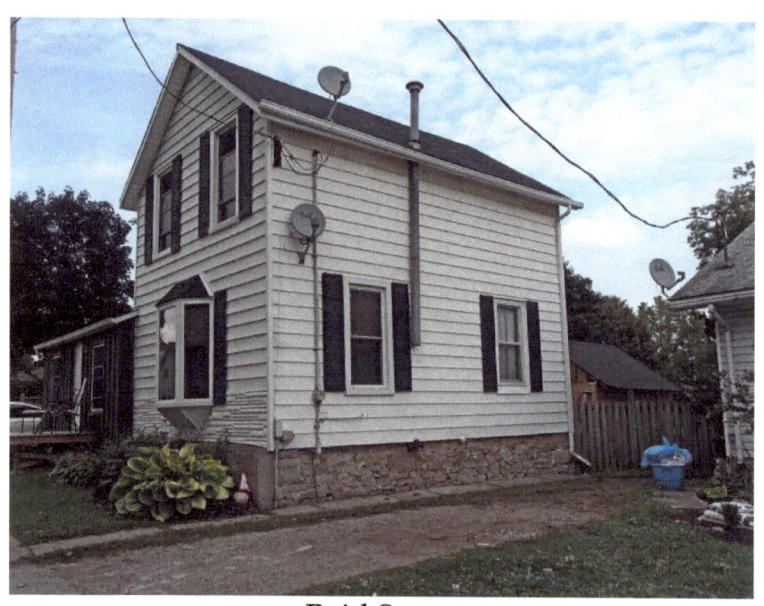

Reid Street

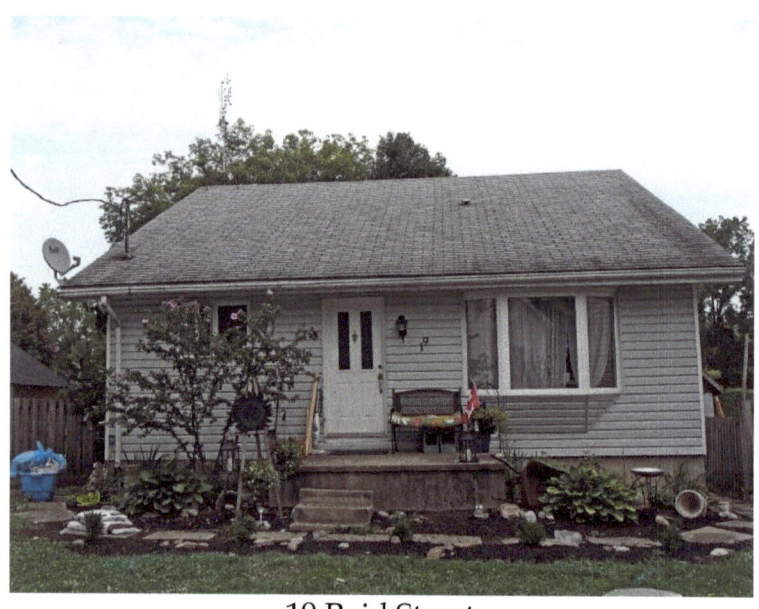

19 Reid Street

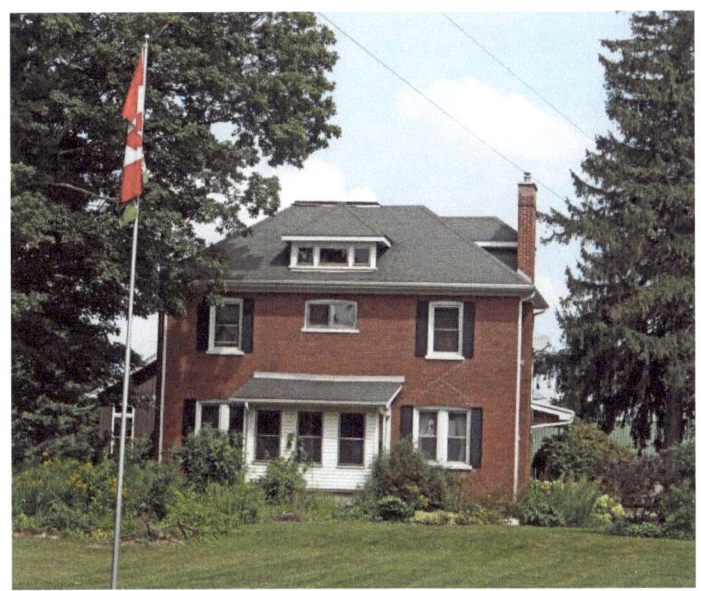

356 St. George Road – hipped roof with dormers

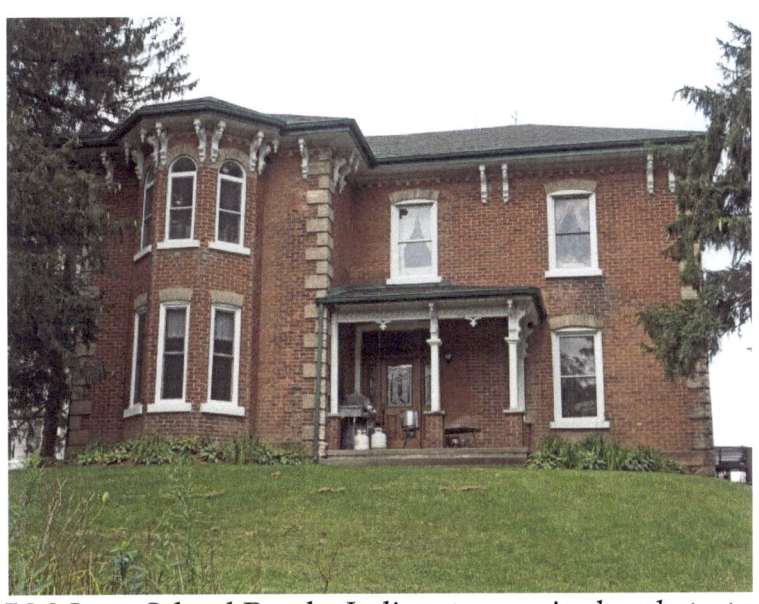

125 McLean School Road – Italianate, cornice brackets, two-storey bay window, corner quoins

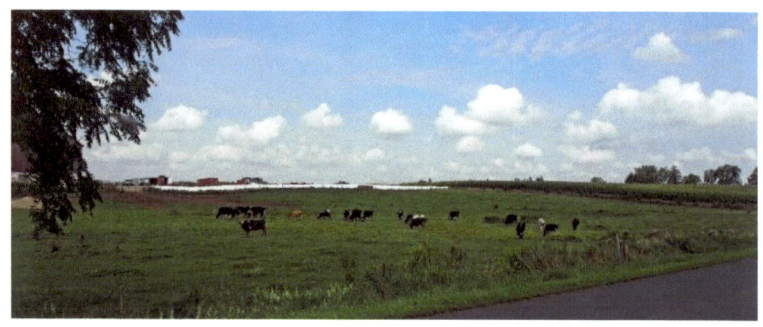

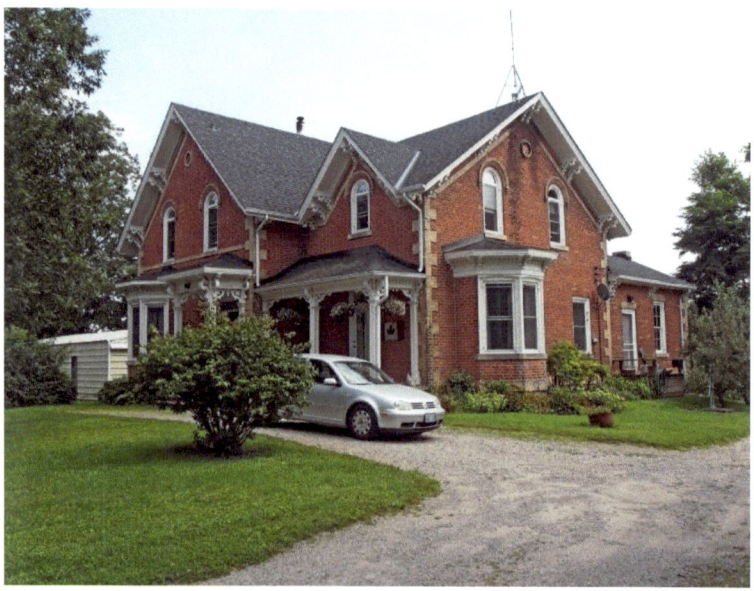

86 McLean School Road – Smith I. Wait House – circa 1875 – High Victorian and Italianate – three layers of brick for the main part of the house and a two-feet thick stone foundation - cornice brackets, corner quoins, bay window

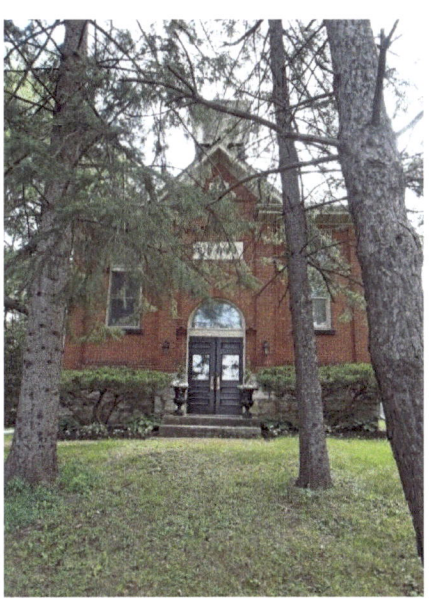

98 McLean School Road – Bruce's School S.S. No. 13 – 1909 – This school was named after a successful Dublin University graduate, James Bruce who taught here for ten years. The one-room schoolhouse closed in 1961.

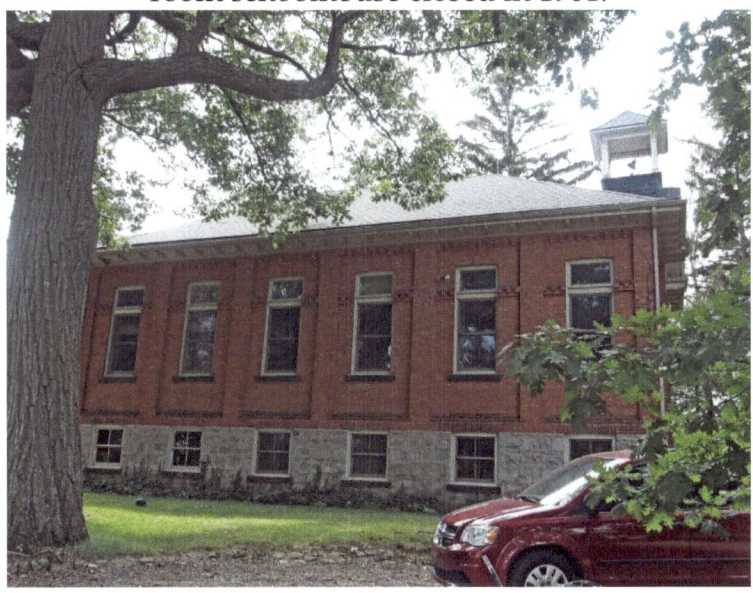

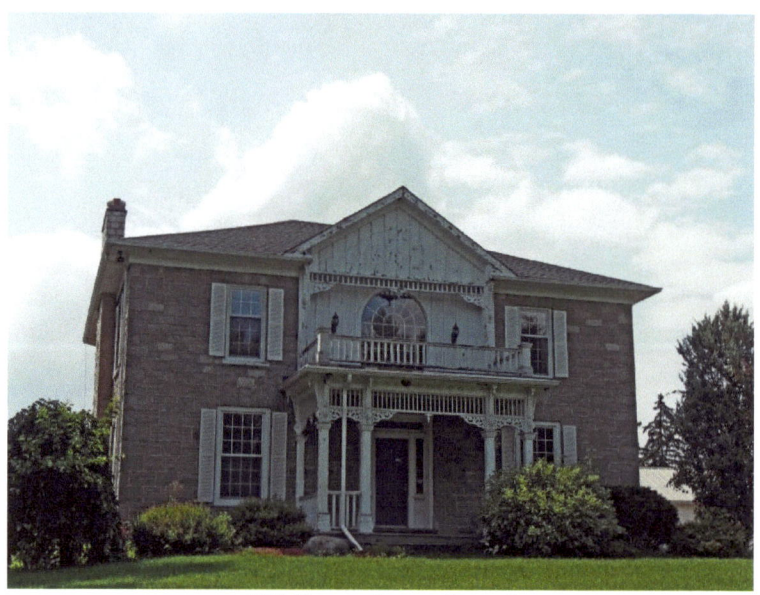

429 Branchton Road

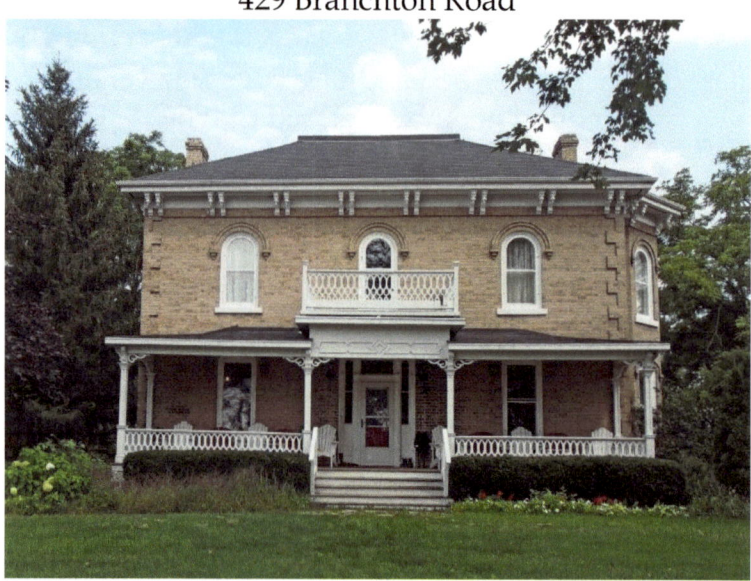

380 Branchton Road – Mayhill Villa/Lewis C. Cope Residence – circa 1867 – Italianate – half-round windows, two sets of original compound chimneys, hipped roof, paired cornice brackets, corner quoins; etched stained glass in the fanlight and sidelights provide an attractive entry

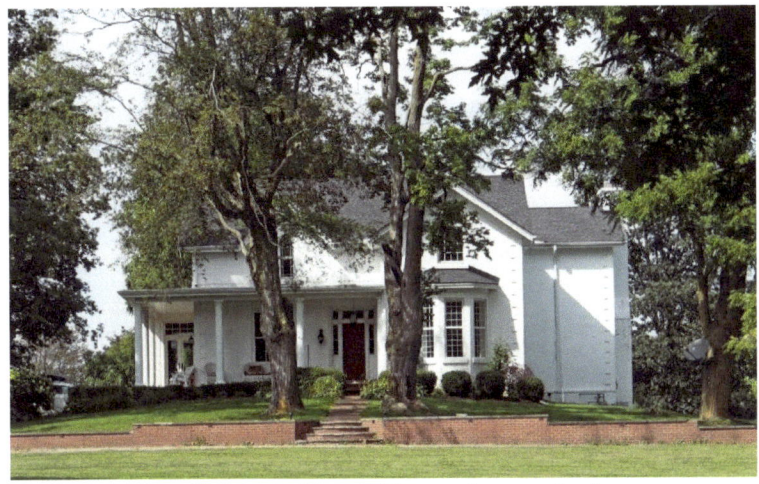

Glen Morris Road East – bay window

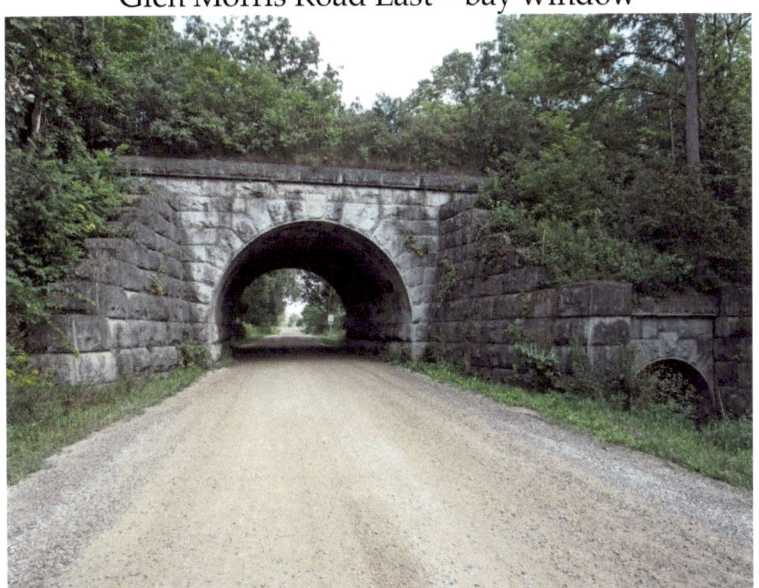

Glen Morris Road East – cut stone railway bridge constructed in 1854 by the Great Western Railway Company over Glen Morris Road East to link Harrisburg with Galt. It is a beautiful example of masonry work with its double arches with keystones which allow both the road and stream to pass under it.

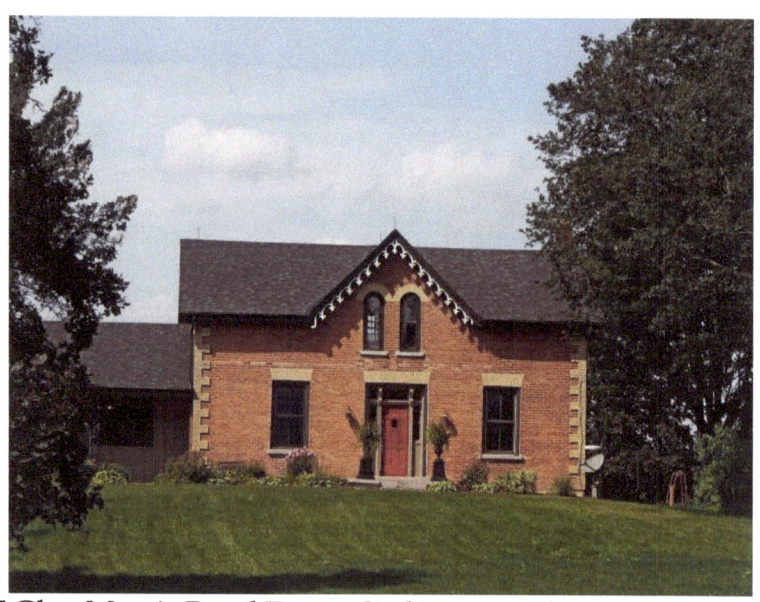

207 Glen Morris Road East – Gothic, verge board trim, quoins

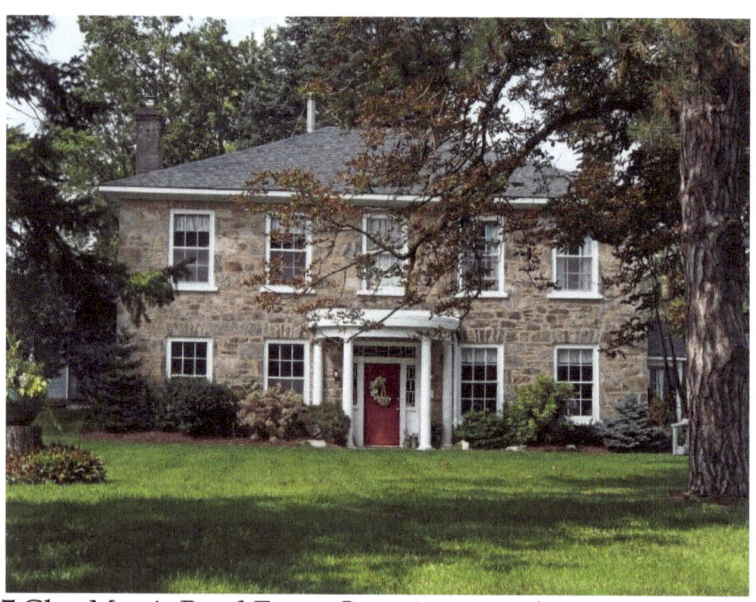

227 Glen Morris Road East – Georgian stone house – six-over-six windows, sidelights and transom

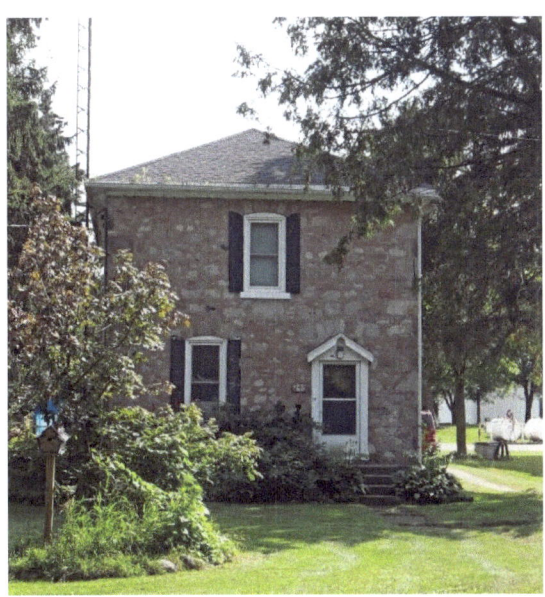

248 Glen Morris Road East – hipped roof, stone building

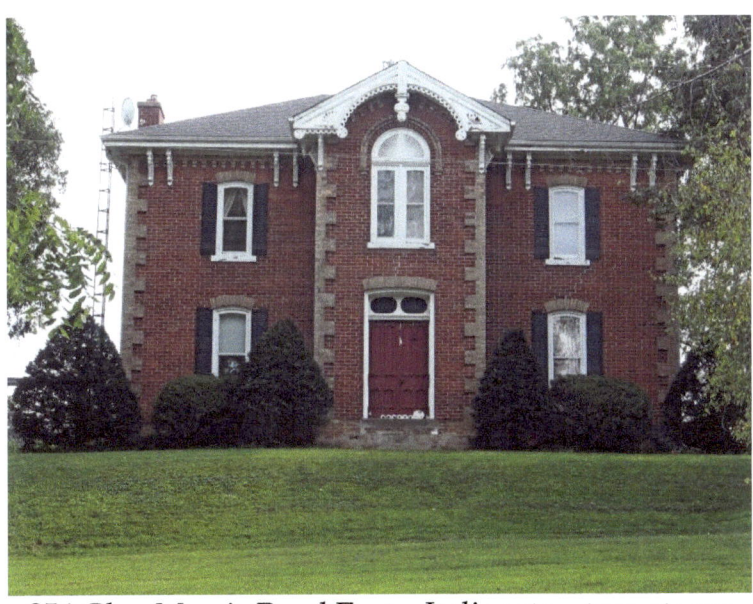

254 Glen Morris Road East – Italianate – two-storey frontispiece, verge board trim and finial on gable, cornice brackets, corner quoins, dentil molding, fanlight

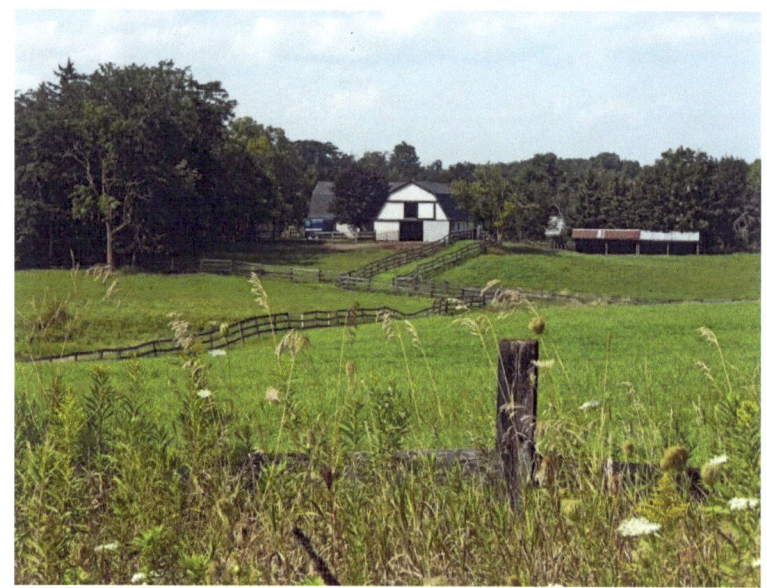
Farm

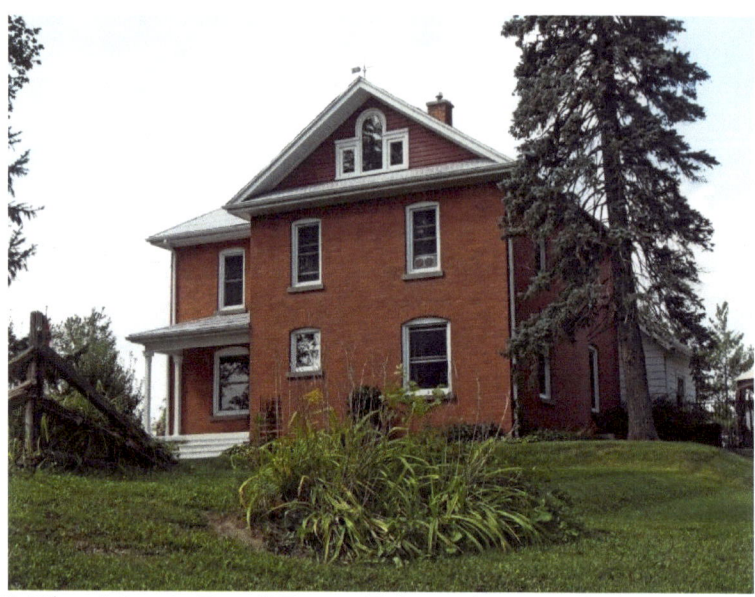
339 Glen Morris Road East – Edwardian, Palladian window

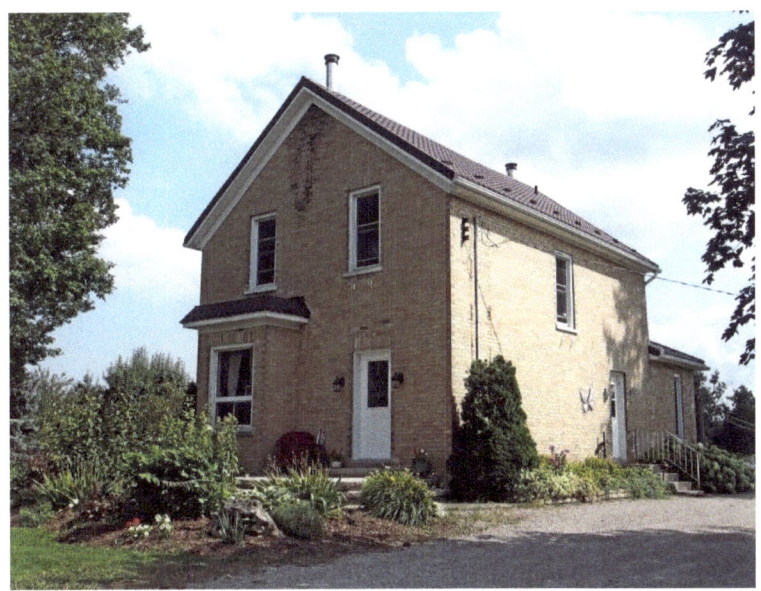

354 Glen Morris Road East – Gothic, bay window

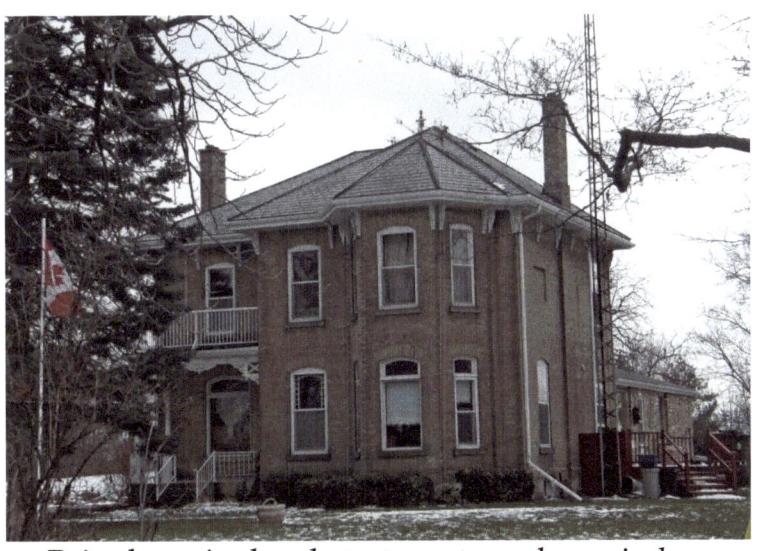

Paired cornice brackets, two-storey bay window

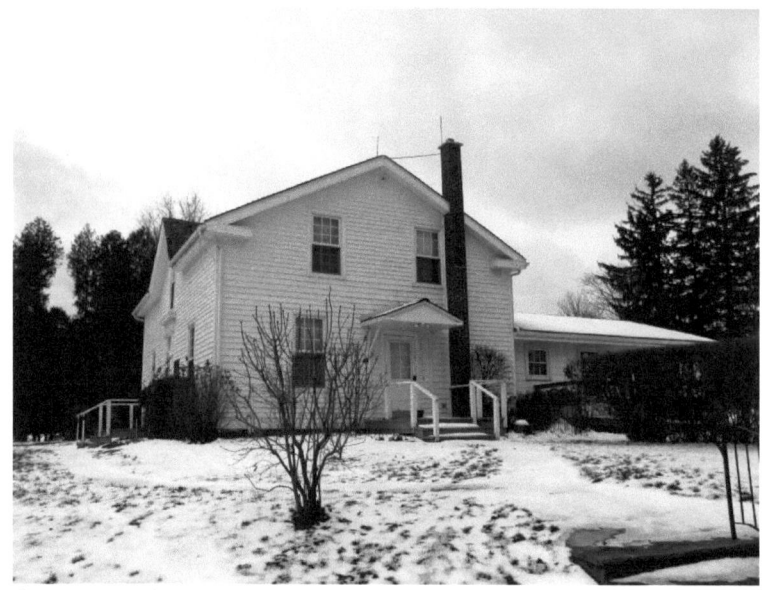

359 Regional Road 35 (Blue Lake Road) – circa 1830 – Neo-Gothic style farmhouse

Adelaide Hoodless was born here in St. George, the youngest of twelve children. Her father died a few months after her birth. Her mother, Jane Hamilton Hunter, was left to manage the farm and a large household. Perhaps the hard work and isolation of her youth inspired Adelaide to take up the cause of domestic reform years later.

After her schooling in a one-room schoolhouse, she stayed with her sister Lizzie while attending 'Ladies College' in Brantford, Ontario. While there, she met John Hoodless who was also the close friend of her sister Lizzie's future husband, Seth Charlton. John Hoodless was the only surviving son of a successful Hamilton furniture manufacturer (Joseph Hoodless). Adelaide married John Hoodless and moved to Hamilton. Adelaide and John had four children: Edna, Muriel, Bernard and John Harold.

Her infant son John Harold died at the age of 14 months, possibly from contaminated milk. Adelaide wanted to ensure that women had the knowledge to prevent deaths like those of her son and she devoted herself to education for new mothers.

She became the second president of the Hamilton branch of the Young Women's Christian Association (YWCA), a role she used to work towards the establishment of domestic science education, and taught classes in domestic science (home economics).

In January 1897, the Minister of Education asked Adelaide to write a textbook for Domestic Science courses. In 1898 she published a book *Public School Domestic Science*. This became known as the 'Little Red Book'. It stressed the importance of hygiene, cleanliness and frugality.

Adelaide travelled all over the province speaking on the subject of domestic science. She was a lively and engaging speaker: "Is it of greater importance that a farmer should know more about the scientific care of his sheep and cattle, than a farmer's wife should know how to care for her family?"

Mr. Erland Lee, of Stoney Creek, heard Adelaide speak, and her message resonated with him. He asked Adelaide to speak at his Farmer's Institute Ladies Night meeting, on February 12, 1897. When she spoke that night, she suggested forming a group with a purpose to broaden the knowledge of domestic science and agriculture as well as to socialize. Adelaide returned one week later to find one hundred and one women in attendance. This group became the first branch of the Women's Institute, with Adelaide as honorary president. Within a decade more than five hundred branches were organized across Canada.

Adelaide met Lady Aberdeen through her work with the National Council for Women. Concerned about families living in isolated surroundings with little or no access to medical care, Lady Aberdeen sought Adelaide's support. Adelaide worked with Lady Aberdeen to found the National Council of Women of Canada, the Victorian Order or Nurses and the National Association of the YWCA.

By October of 1902, the Ministry of Education was going to make domestic science a regular part of curriculum in Ontario schools. Adelaide had her sights on the next step. She wanted Domestic Science to be offered at the university level. She also knew she needed a wealthy patron to finance the project. She approached Sir William MacDonald, a wealthy Montreal non-smoker, who had made his money in tobacco. She persuaded him to fund two programs – one in Ontario and one in Quebec.

The University of Guelph recognizes her contribution to education by hanging her portrait in what was once called the MacDonald Institute. (I attended Grade 7 here when it was called Macdonald Consolidated School). It now operates as a museum.

In 1911, the year after she died, one of Hamilton's new schools was named after her. (Zane, our oldest son, attended here for a year).

Bethel Road

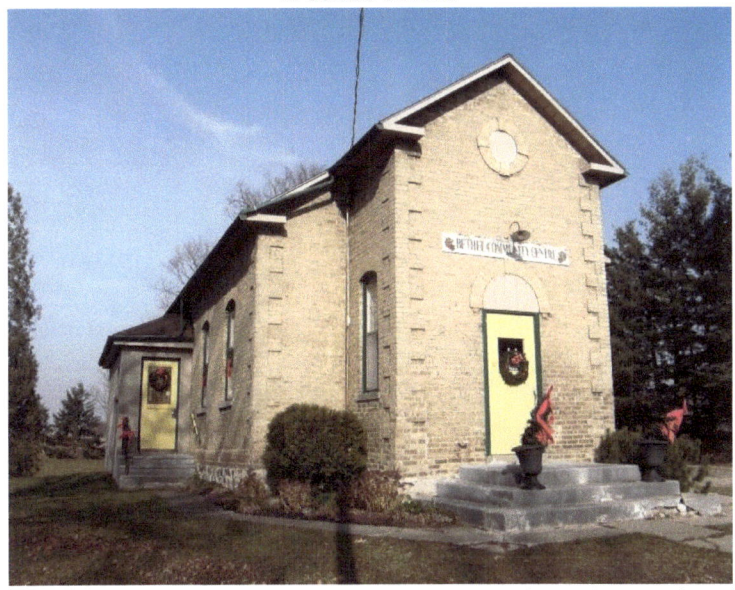

157 Bethel Road – Perley School – 1844 – The white school was built in Italianate style complete with quoins and elliptical arches over the windows.

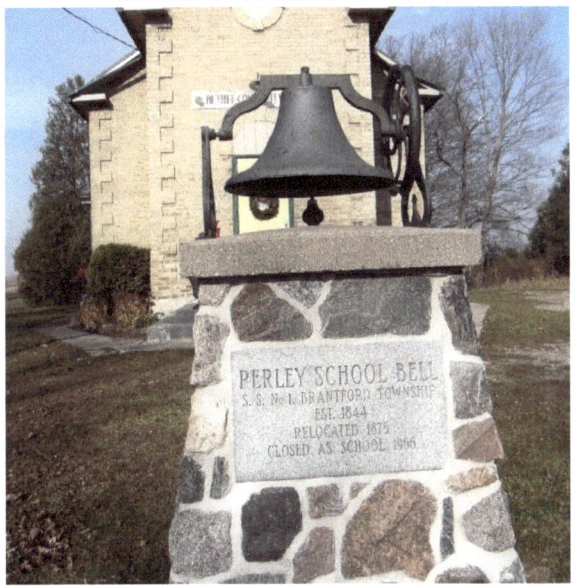

Perley School Bell was placed on the cairn in front of the school when it was closed in 1966.

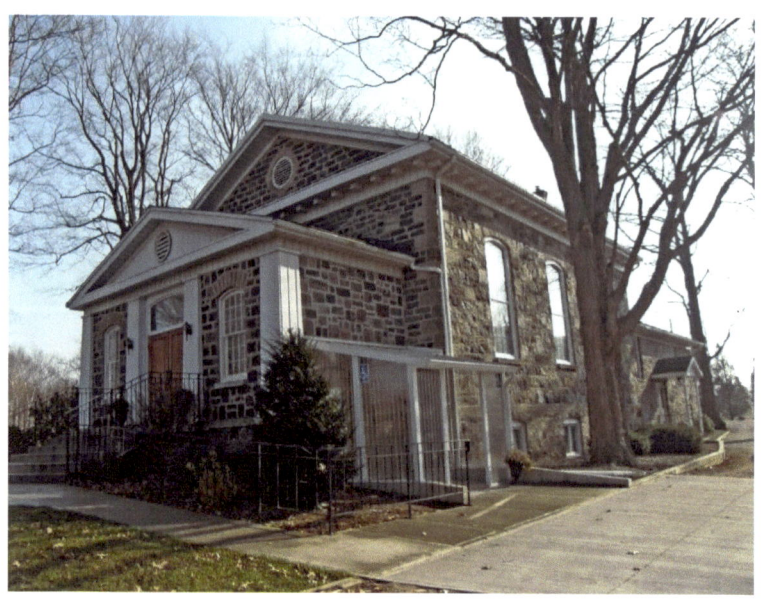

154 Bethel Road – Bethel Stone United Church – 1864 – built from local stone gathered from the fields – Classical Revival style with elliptical arches over the 12-over-12 windows

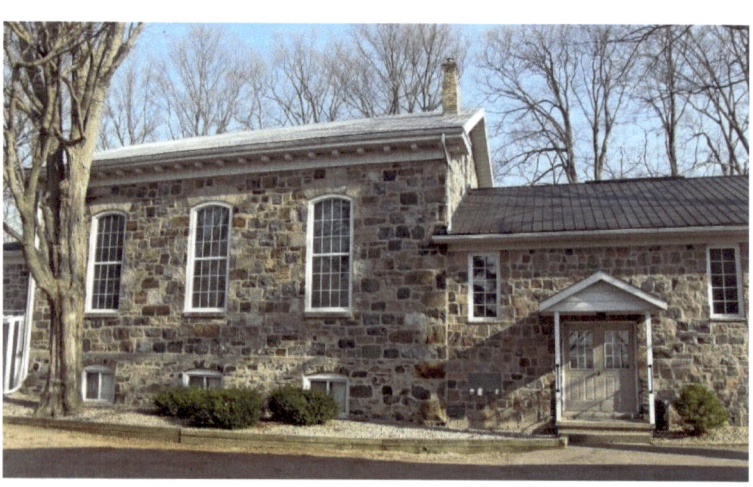

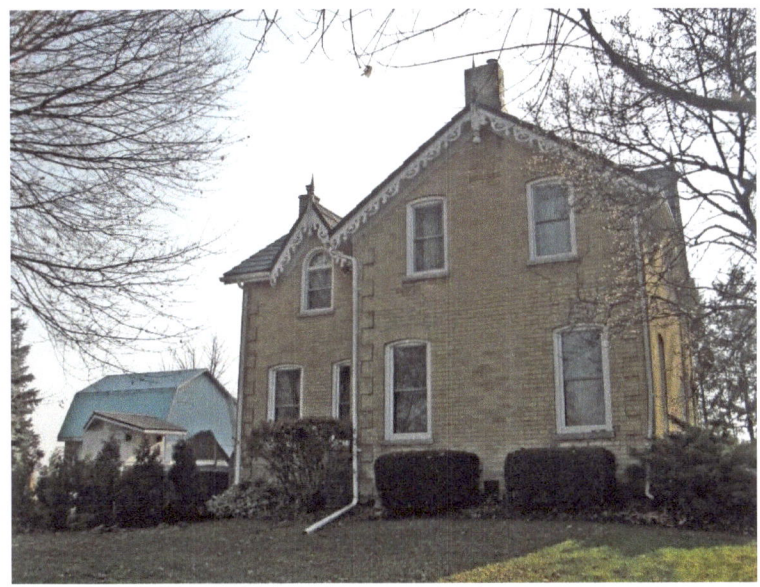

Bethel Road – Gothic – verge board trim and finials on gables, corner quoins

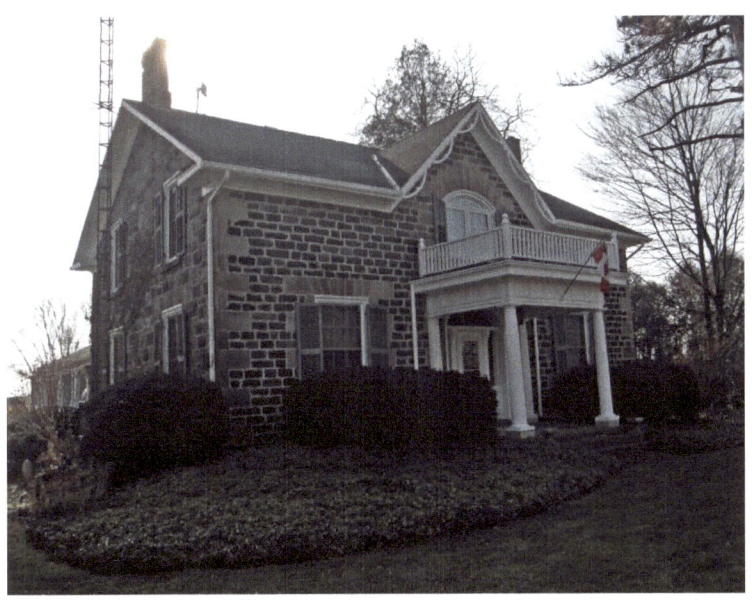

Bethel Road – Gothic – verge board trim on gable

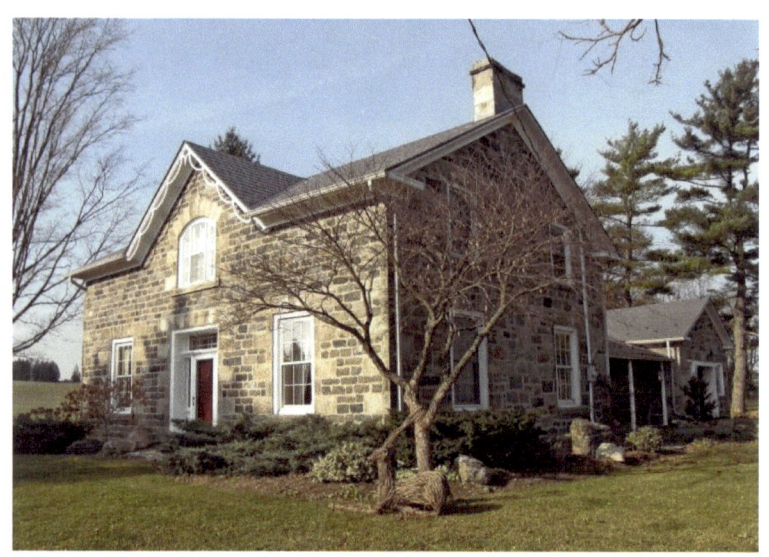

Bethel Road – verge board trim on gable

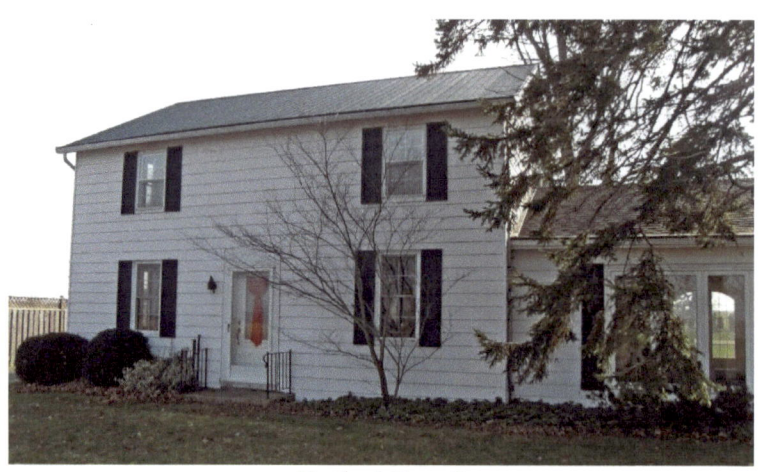

Bethel Road

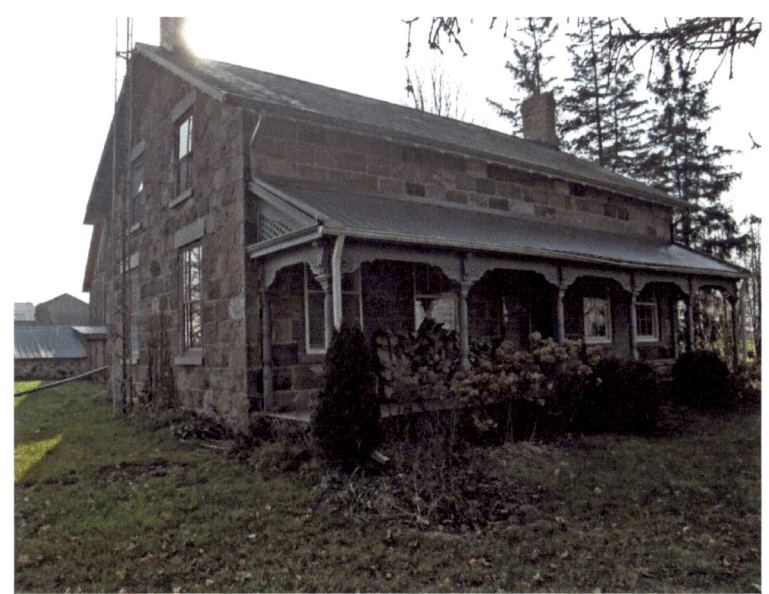

Bethel Road

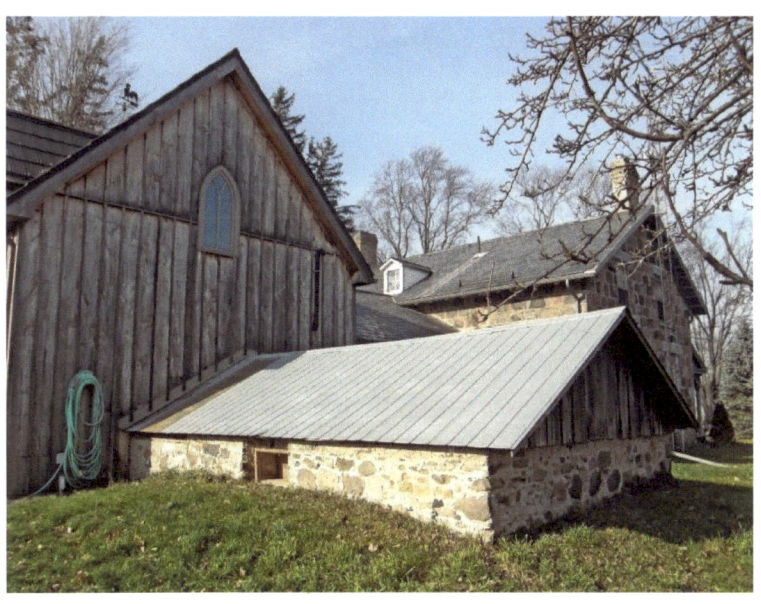

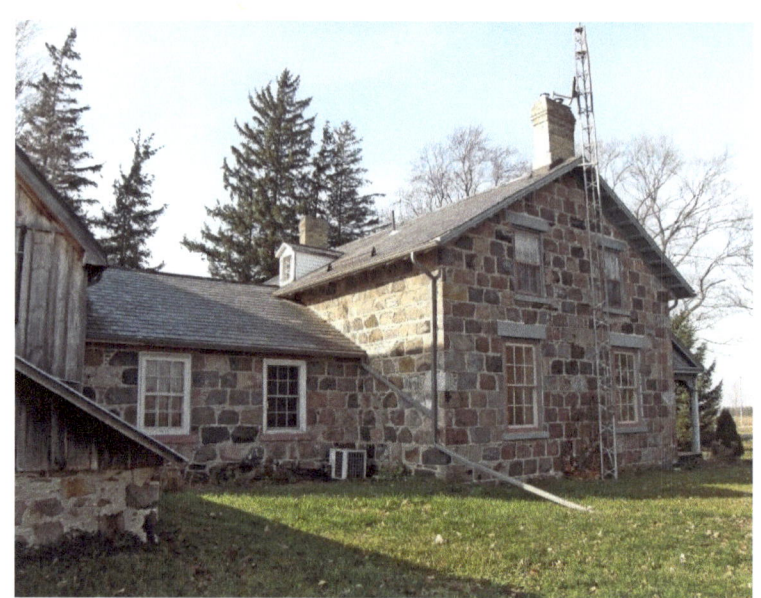

Bethel Road – multi-colored stone

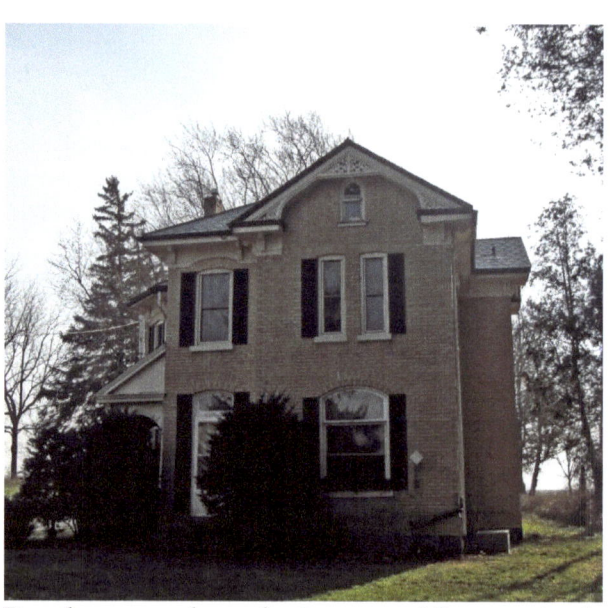

Bethel Road – verge board trim on gable, cornice brackets

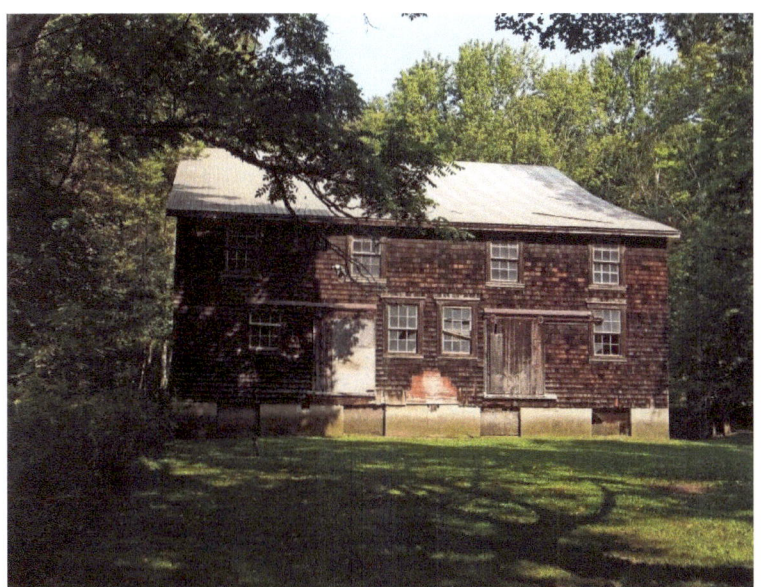

308 Robinson Road – Apps Mill – 1846 – The Apps family operated it as a flour mill using Whiteman Creek for power until 1959 when hurricane Hazel flooded the entire bottom floor. It has horizontal wood siding and six over six windows.

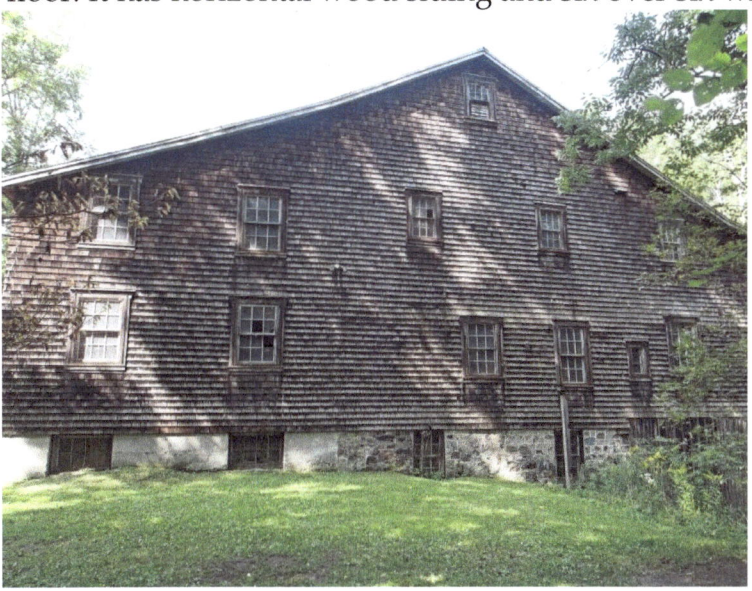

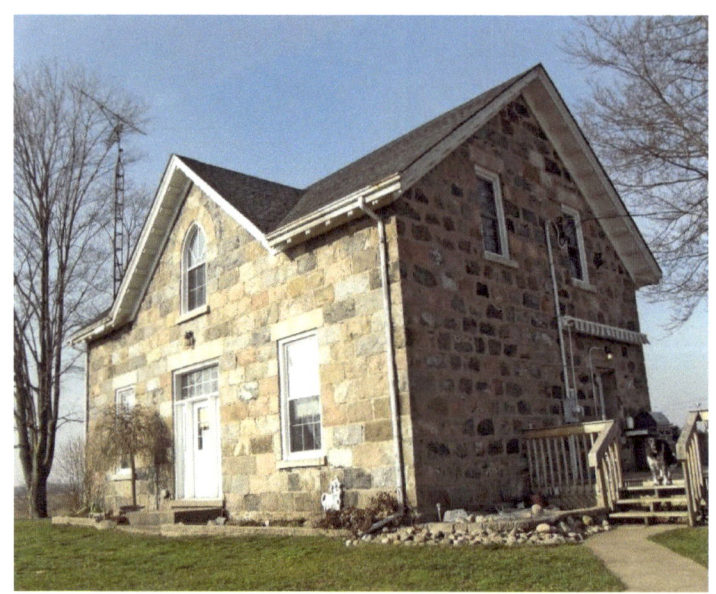
Bethel Road – Gothic Revival – stone

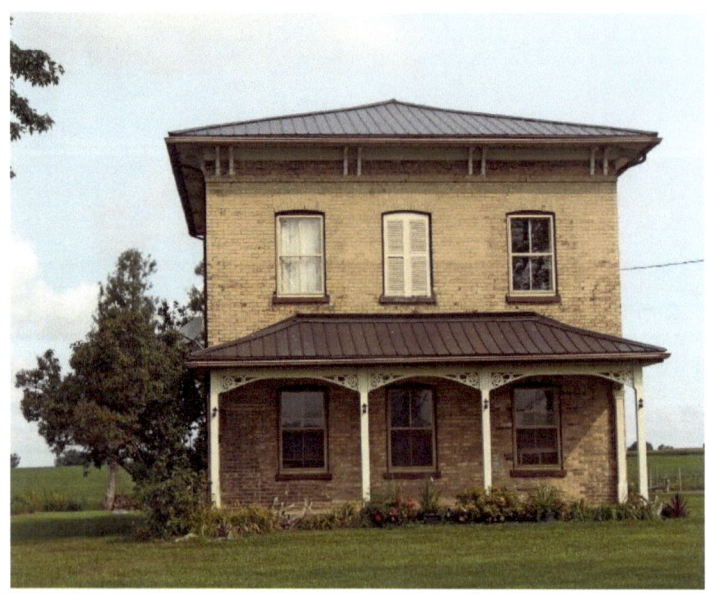
475 Robinson Road – hipped roof, paired cornice brackets

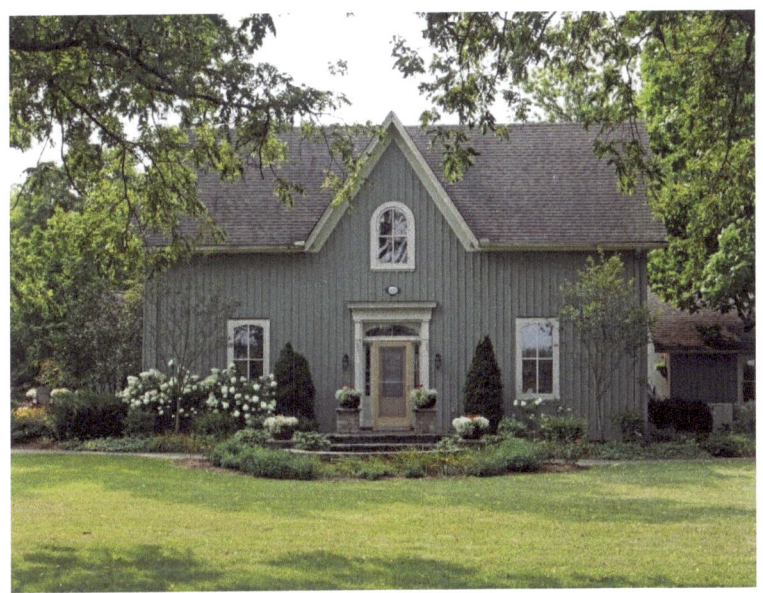

420 Robinson Road – Ontario Cottage

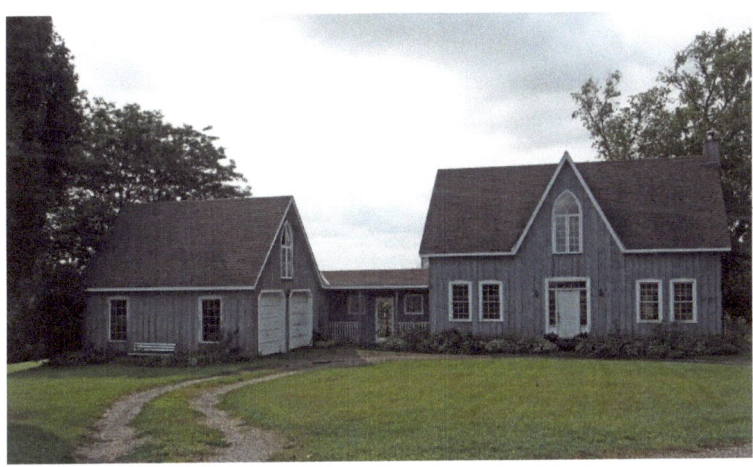

400 Robinson Road – Ontario Cottage

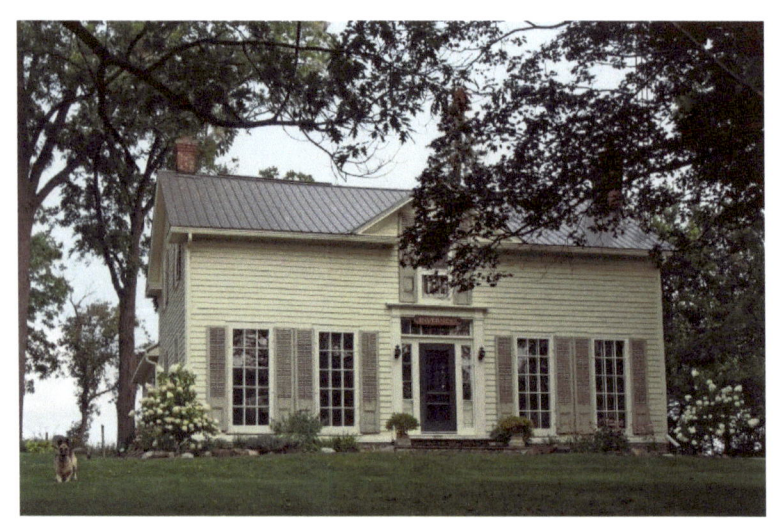

353 Robinson Road – Inverness

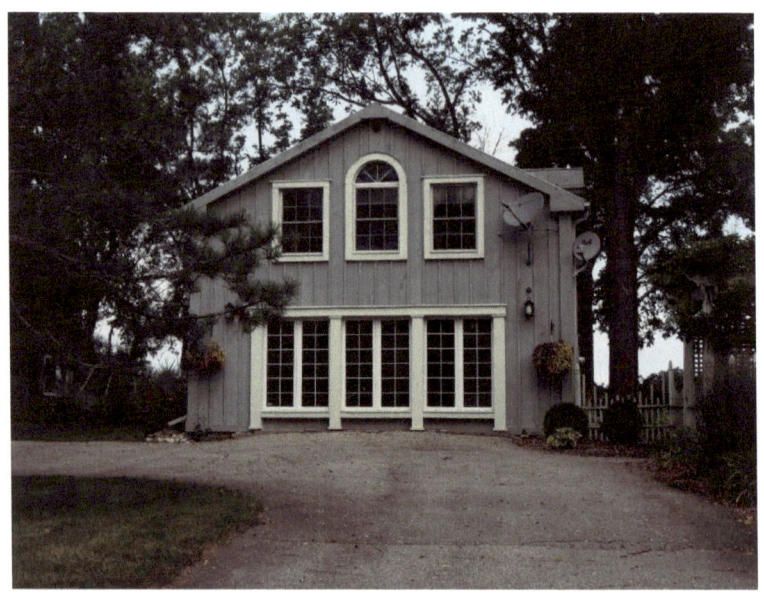

Oakland

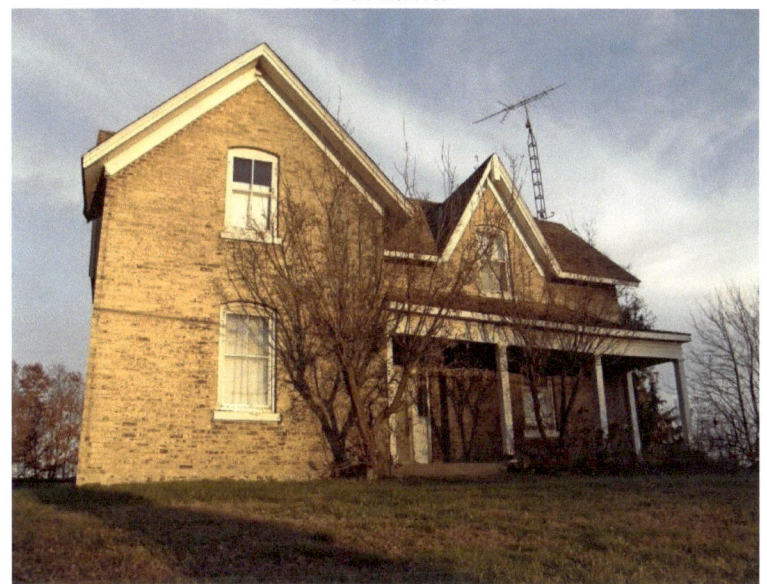

62 King Street South – Gothic Revival

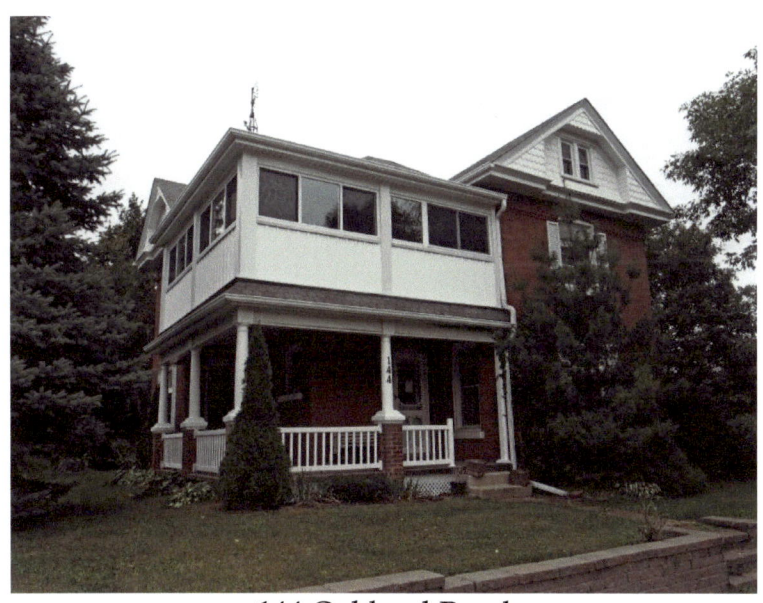

144 Oakland Road

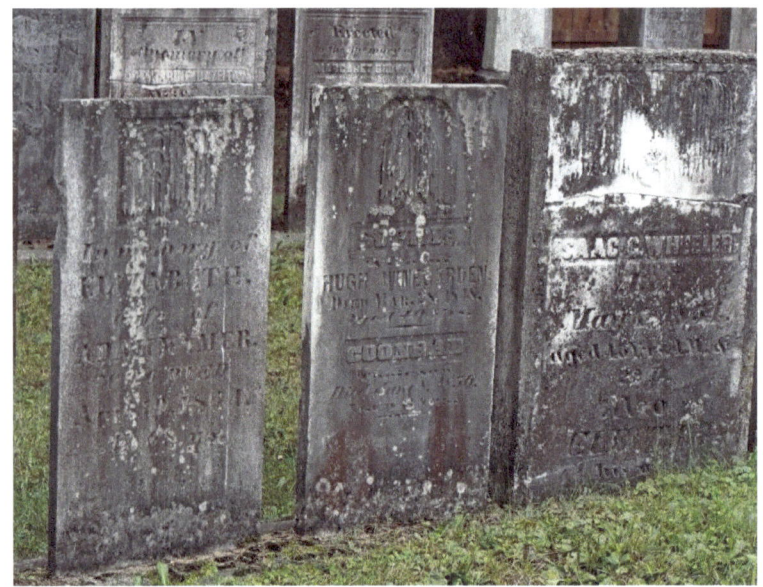

United Empire Loyalists Burial Ground

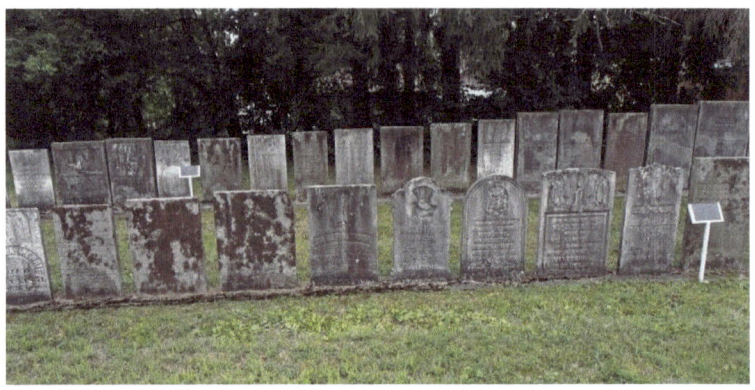

Some gravestones give the date of deaths of 1871 and 1881

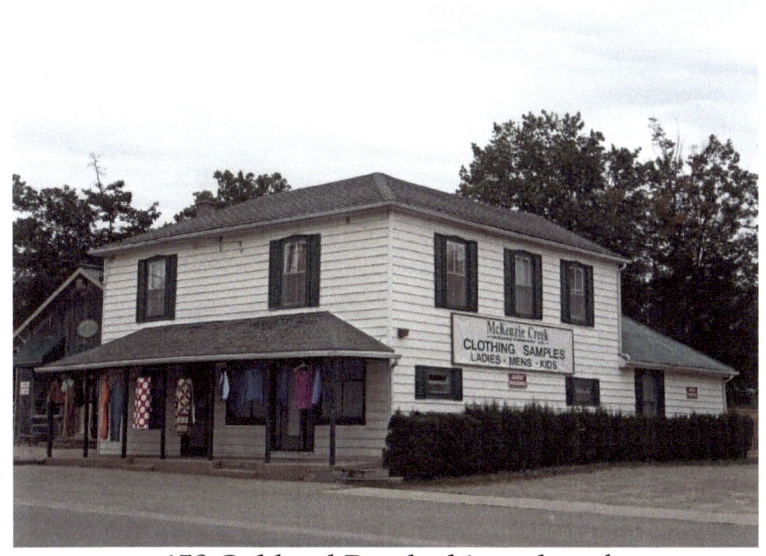

150 Oakland Road – hipped roof

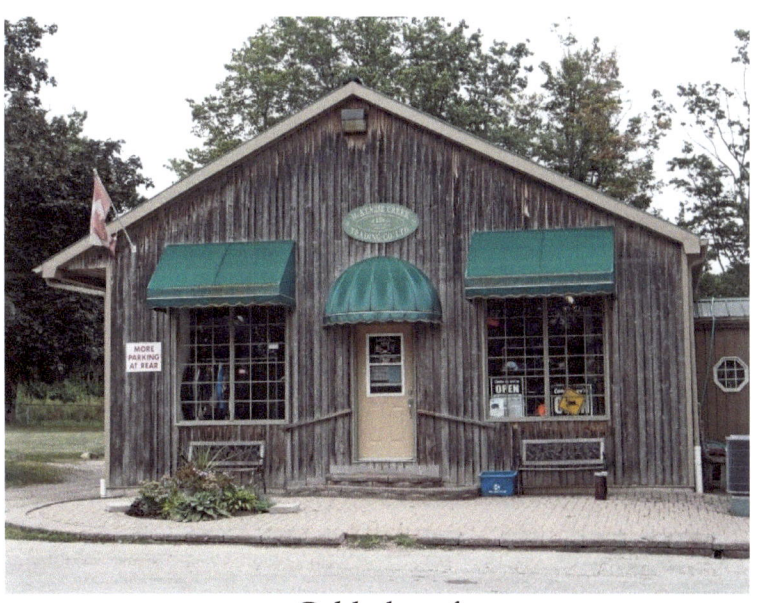

Gabled roof

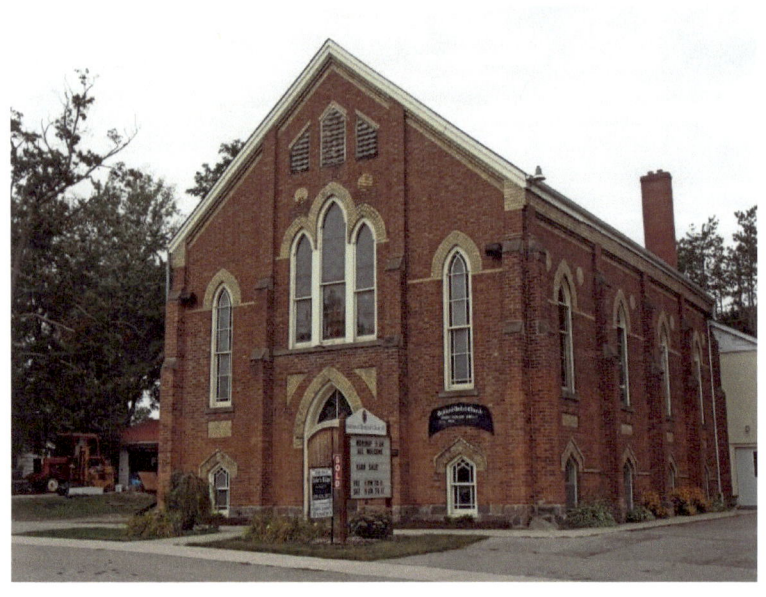

154 Oakland Road – Oakland United Church
(Methodist Church – 1886) – Gothic Revival, lancet windows, dichromatic brickwork, buttresses

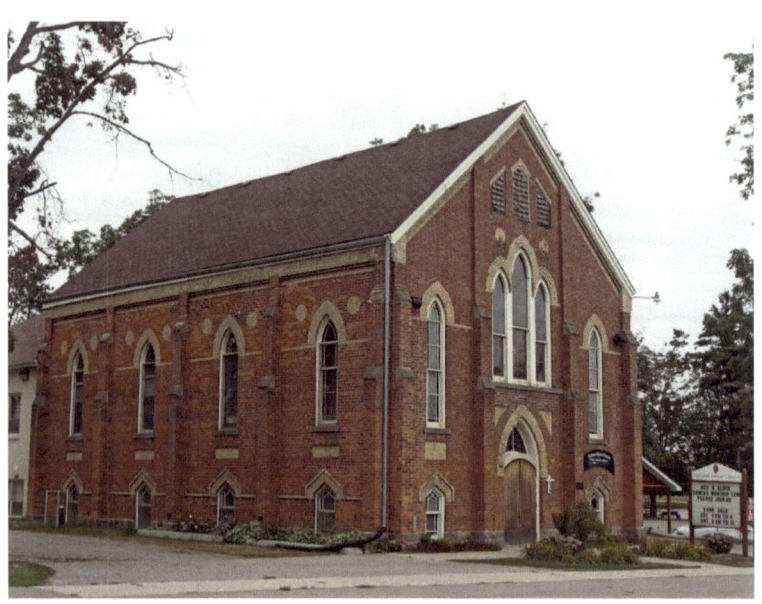

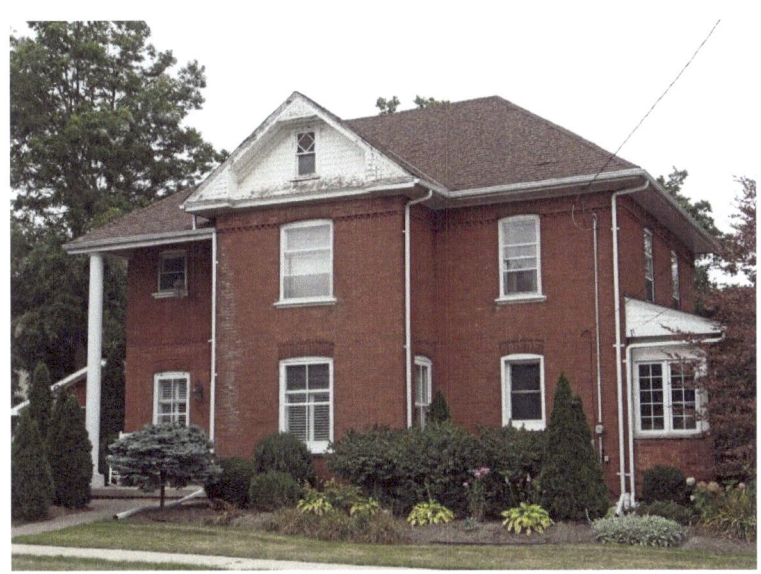
Oakland Road – hipped roof

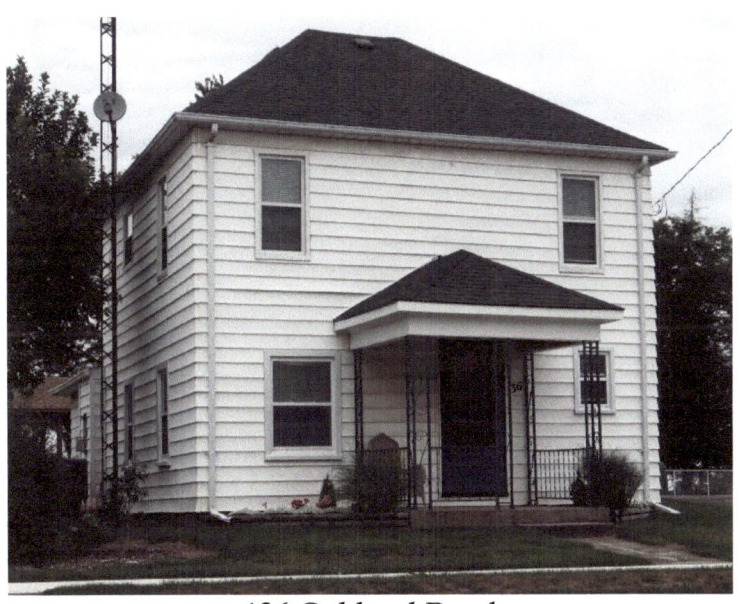
136 Oakland Road

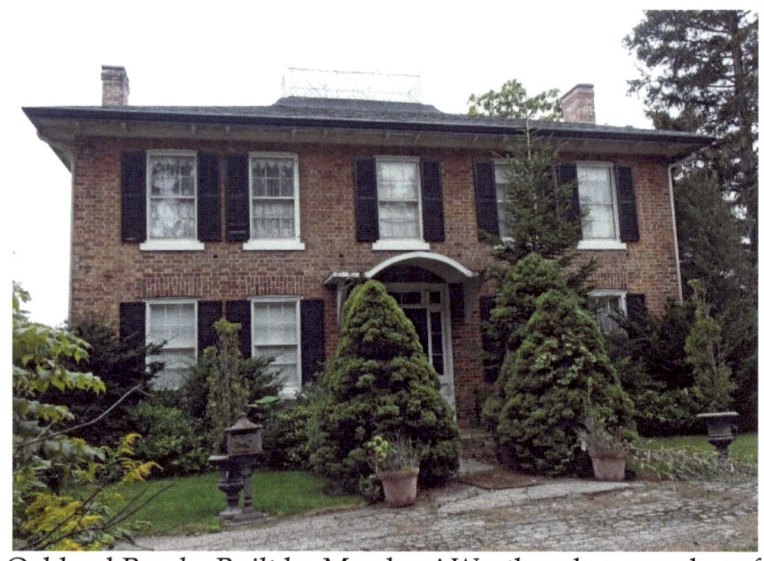

129 Oakland Road – Built by Mordecai Westbrook, a member of one of the original families of Oakland. Georgian style with original double hung six over six windows and shutters. The walls are triple-bricked with bricks said to have been made on site. The widow's walk and rear stone coach house are both original.

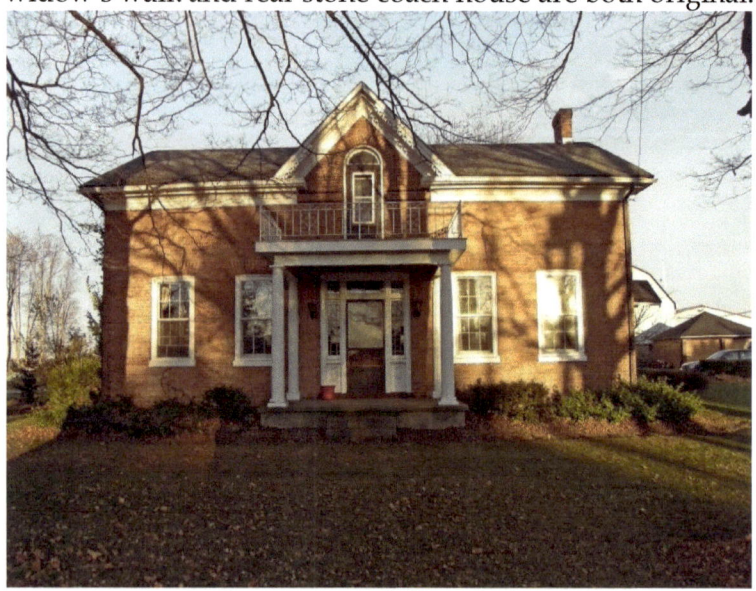

Gothic – second floor balcony

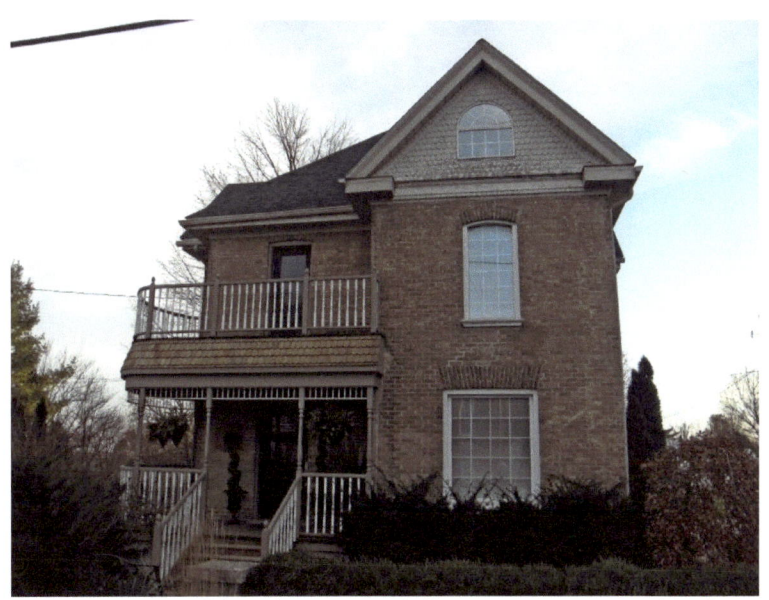

1 Roy Street, Oakland – second floor wraparound balcony, cornice return on gable, window voussoirs

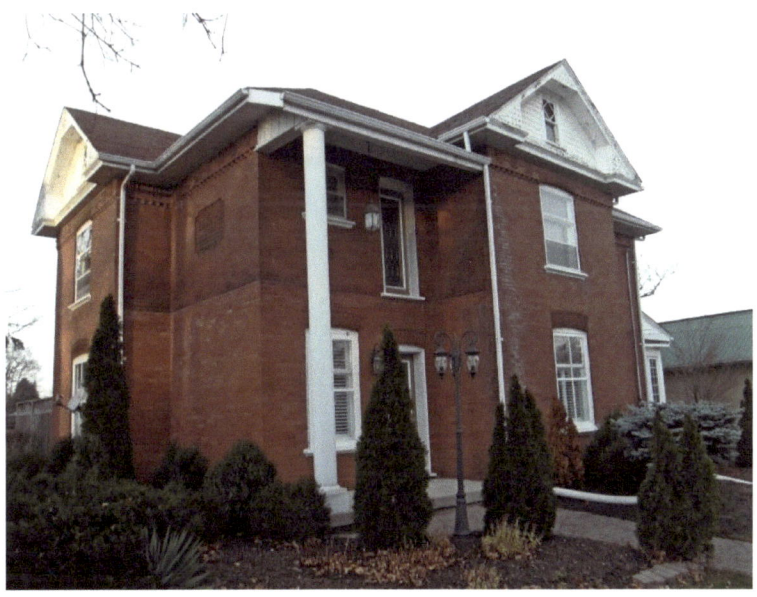

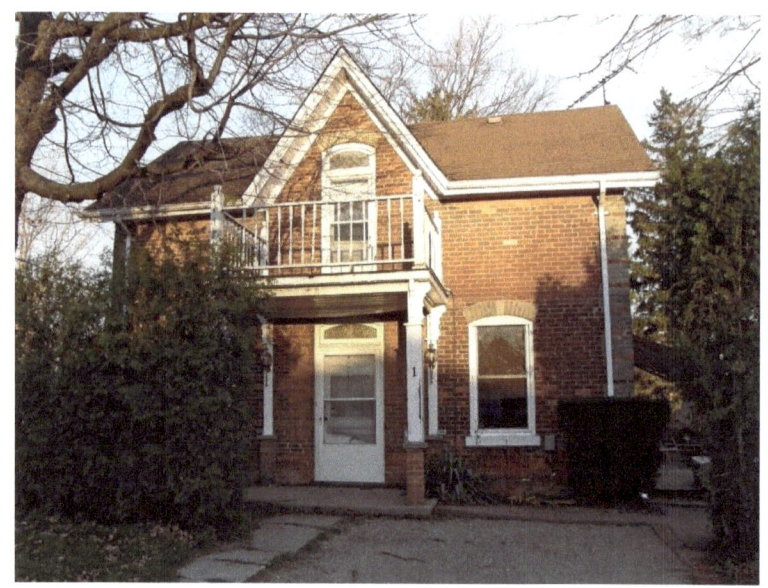

Gothic

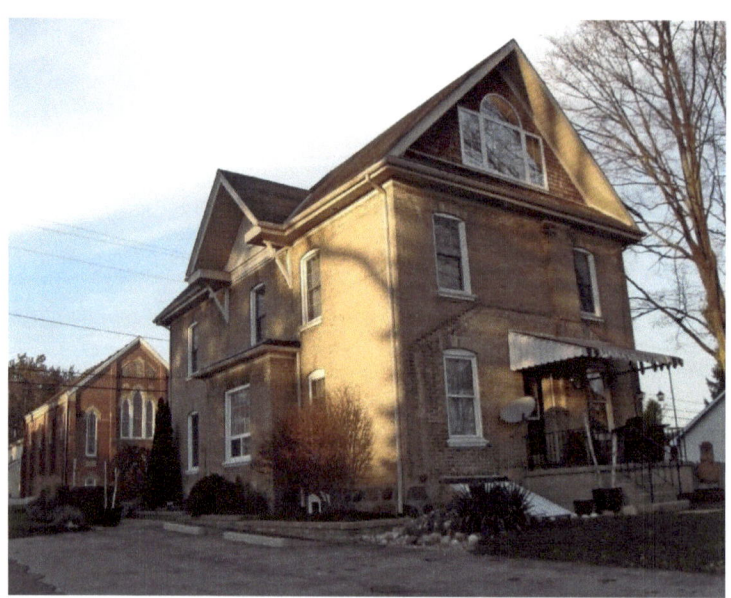

Palladian window in gable

Scotland

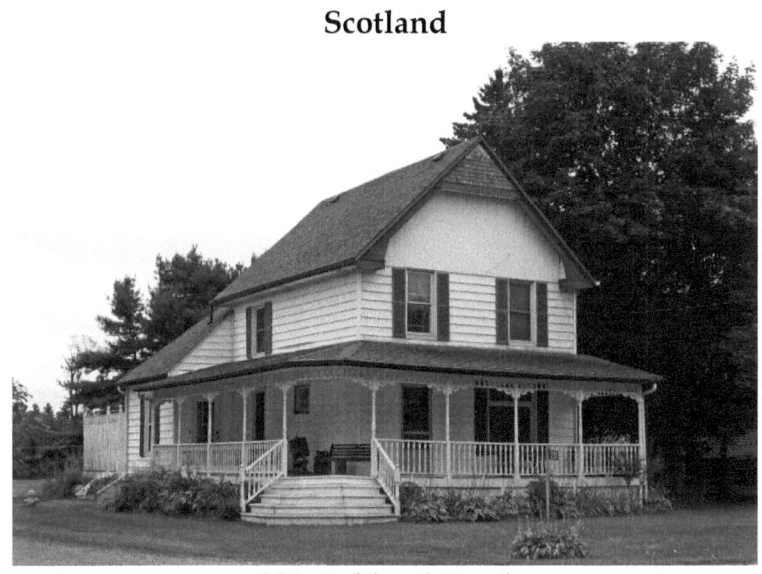

231 Oakland Road

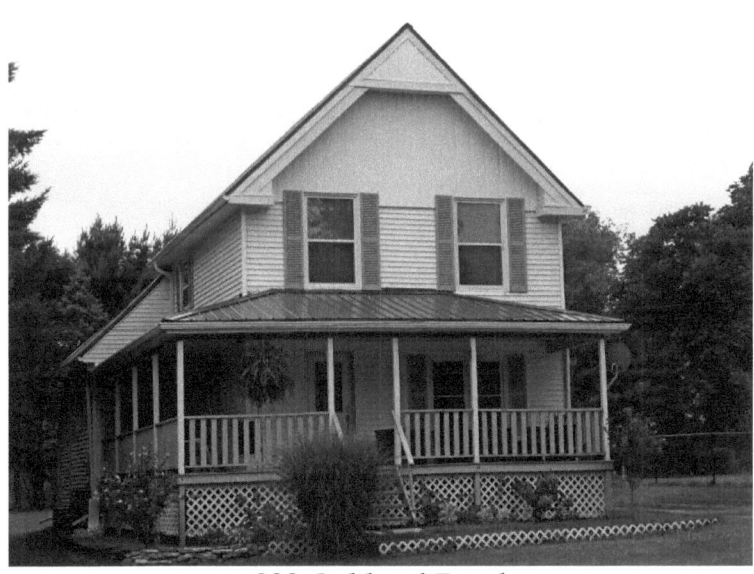

233 Oakland Road

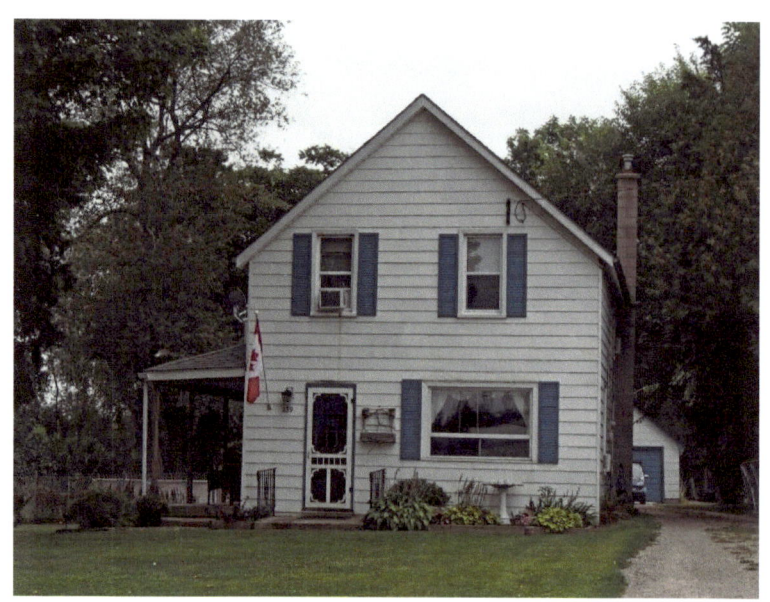

239 Oakland Road

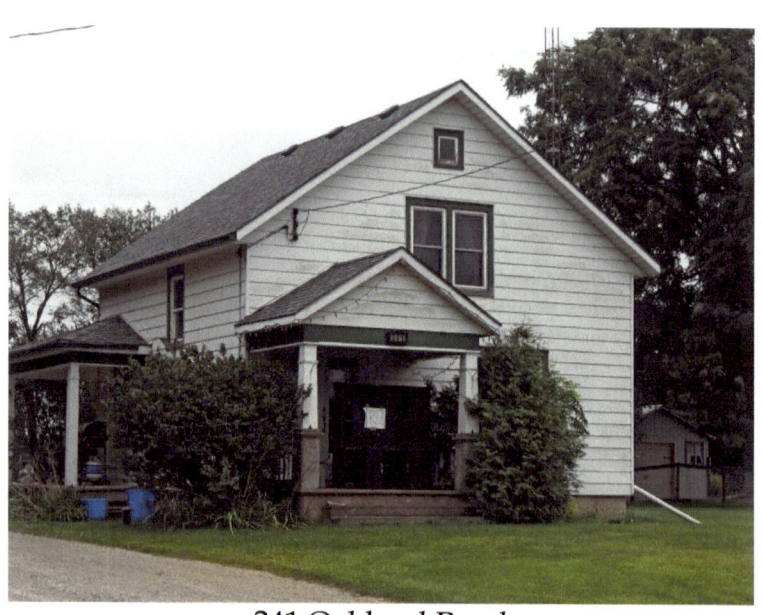

241 Oakland Road

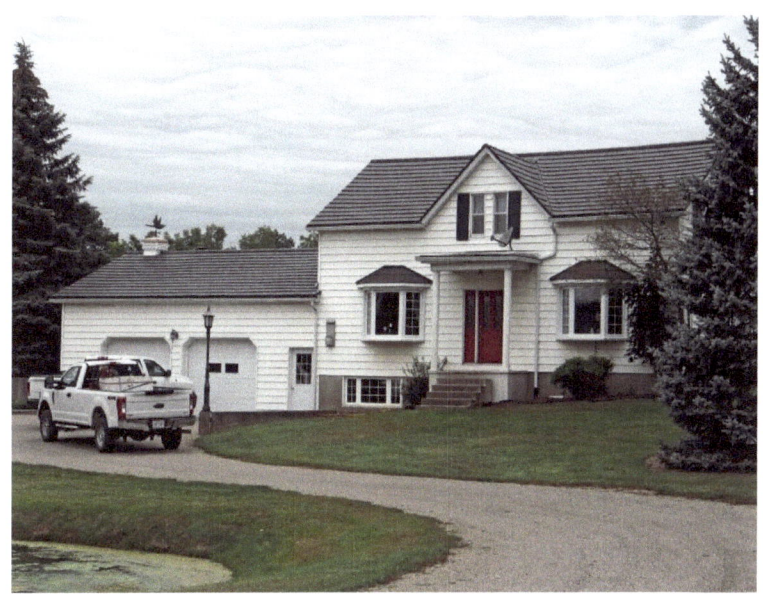

240 Oakland Road

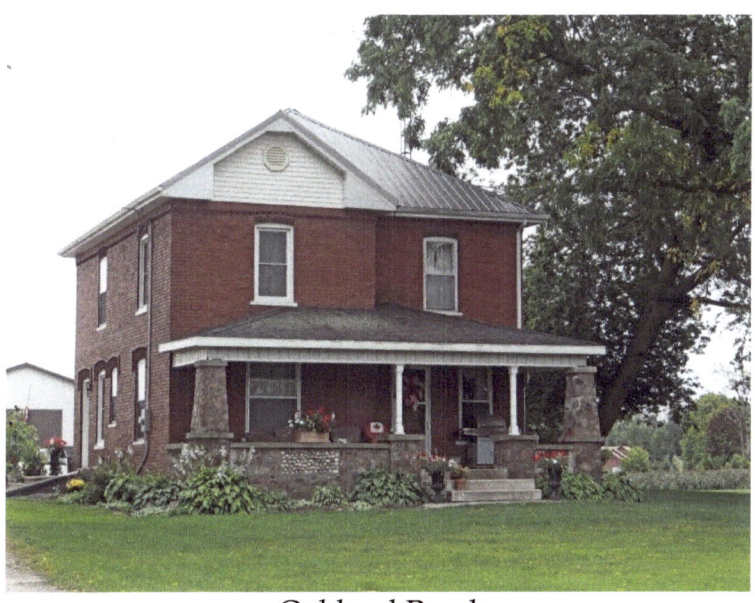

Oakland Road

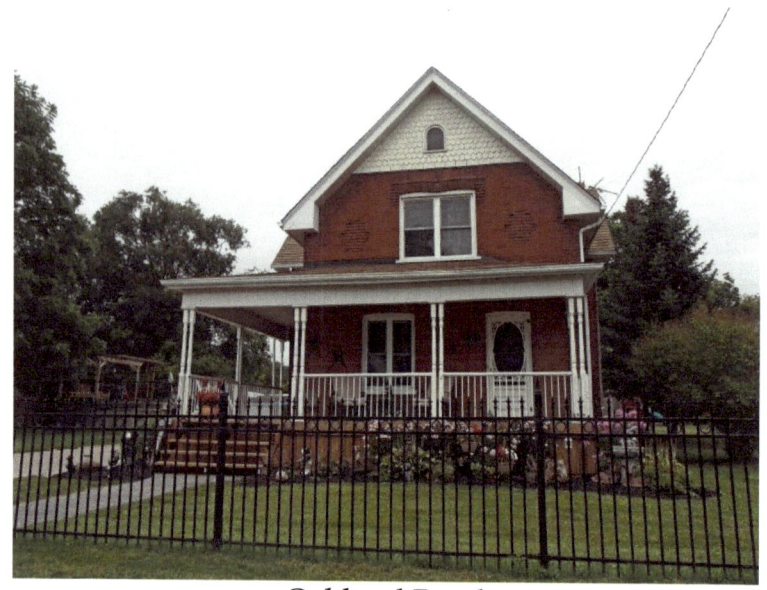

Oakland Road

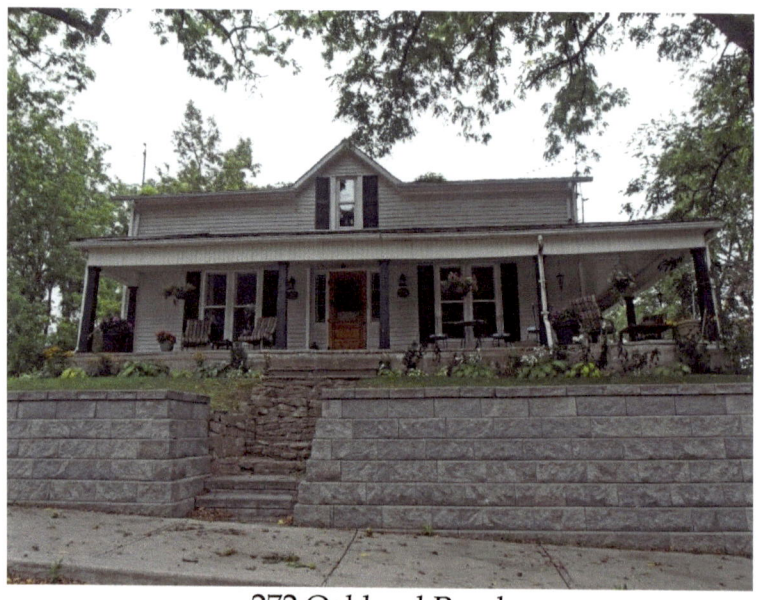

272 Oakland Road

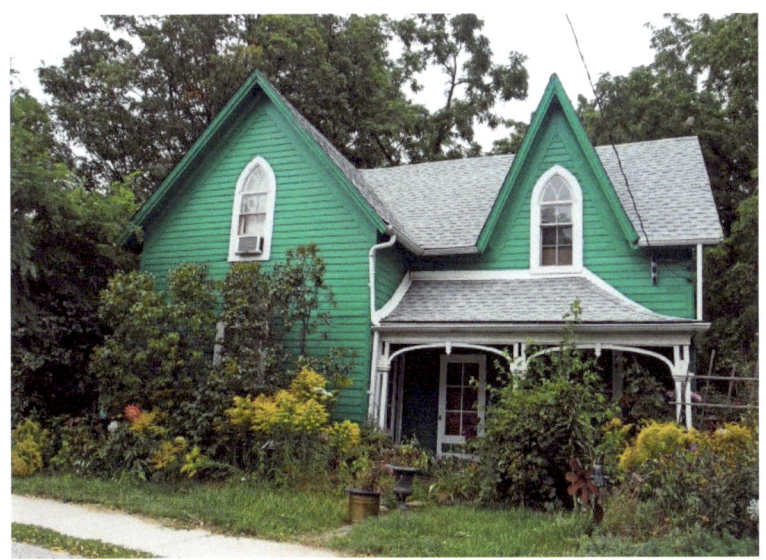

Oakland Road

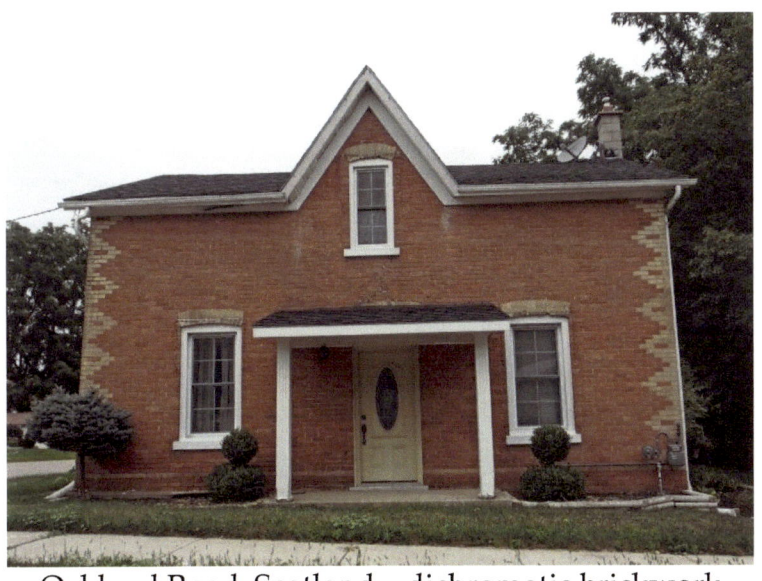

Oakland Road, Scotland – dichromatic brickwork

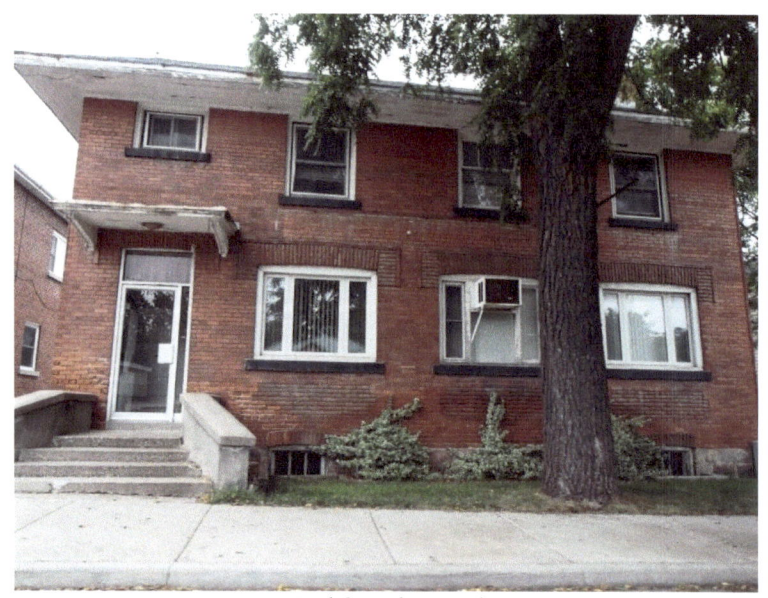

Oakland Road

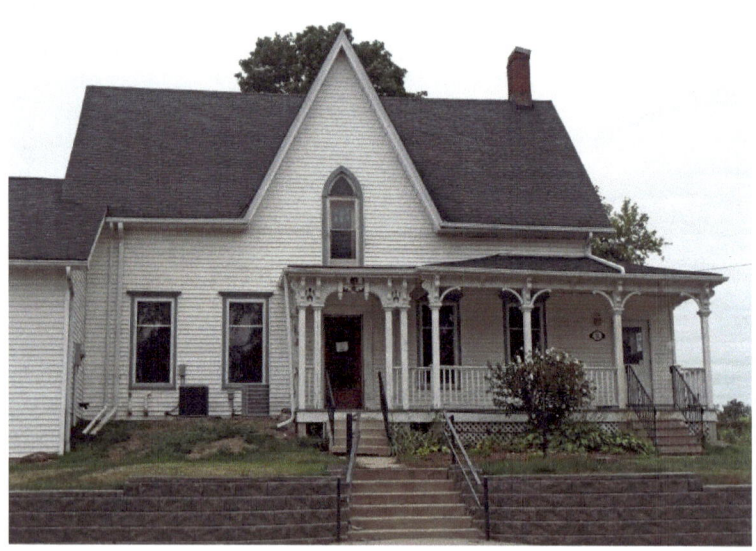

51 Simcoe Street

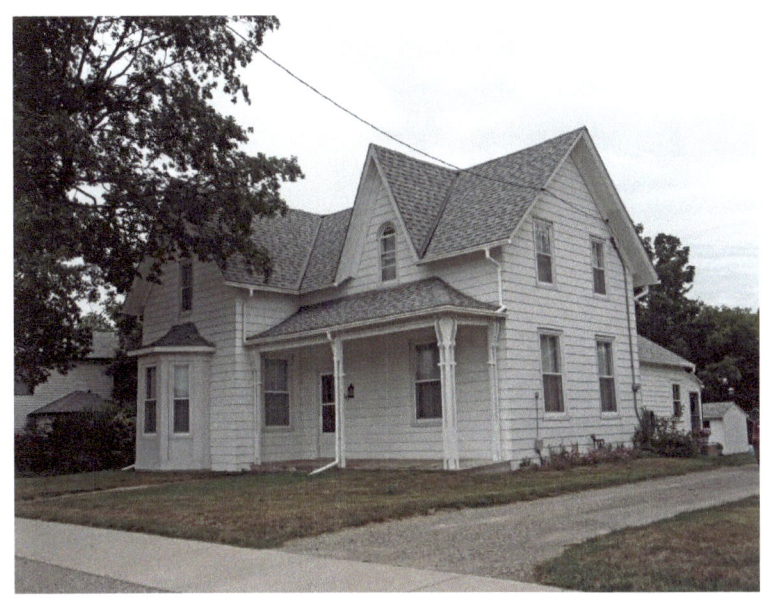

60 Simcoe Street

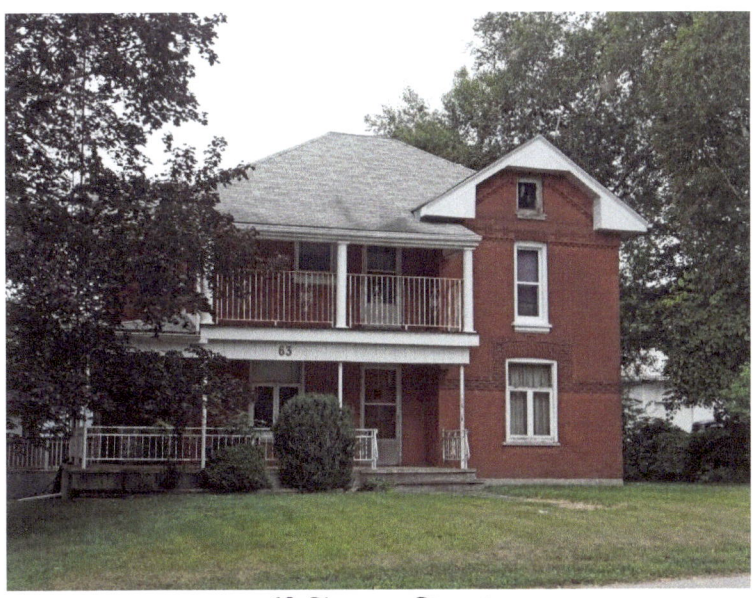

63 Simcoe Street

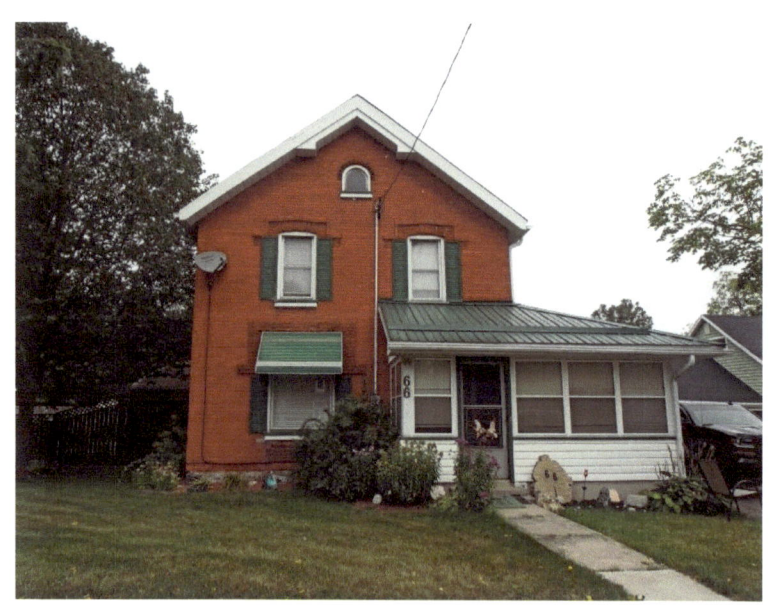

66 Simcoe Street

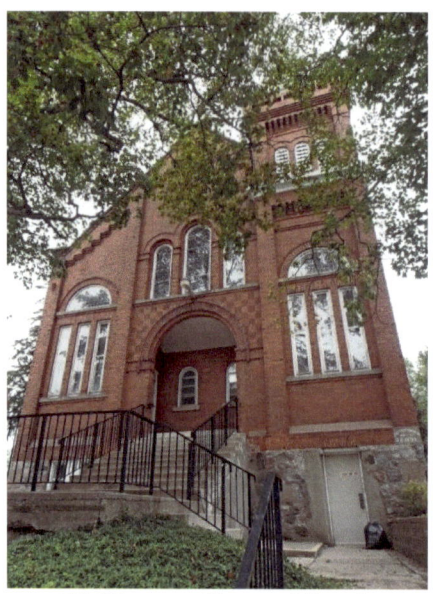

74 Simcoe Street North

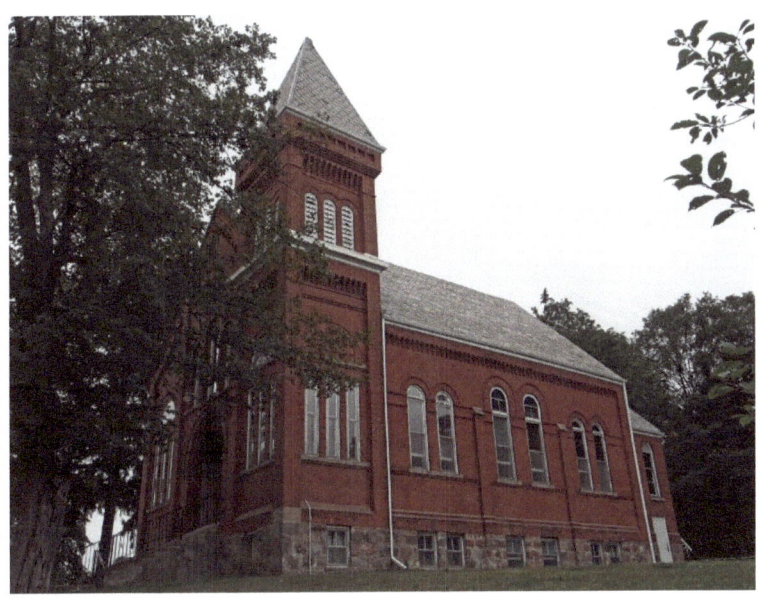

74 Simcoe Street North - Scotland Baptist Church – July 17, 1894 A.D. - Romanesque

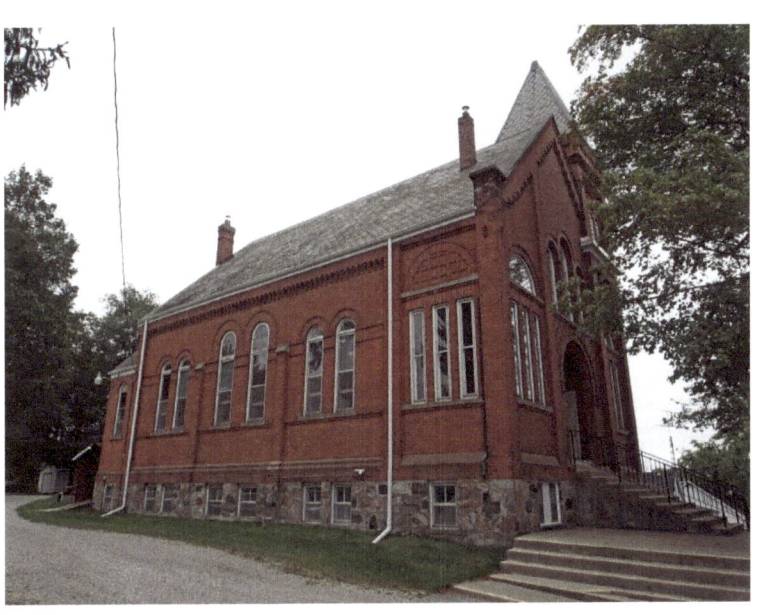

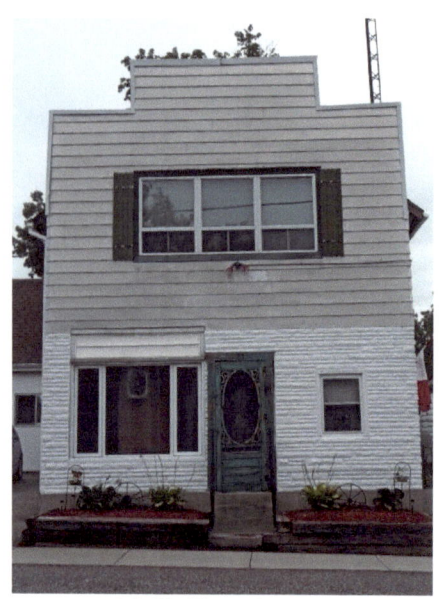

33 Talbot Street

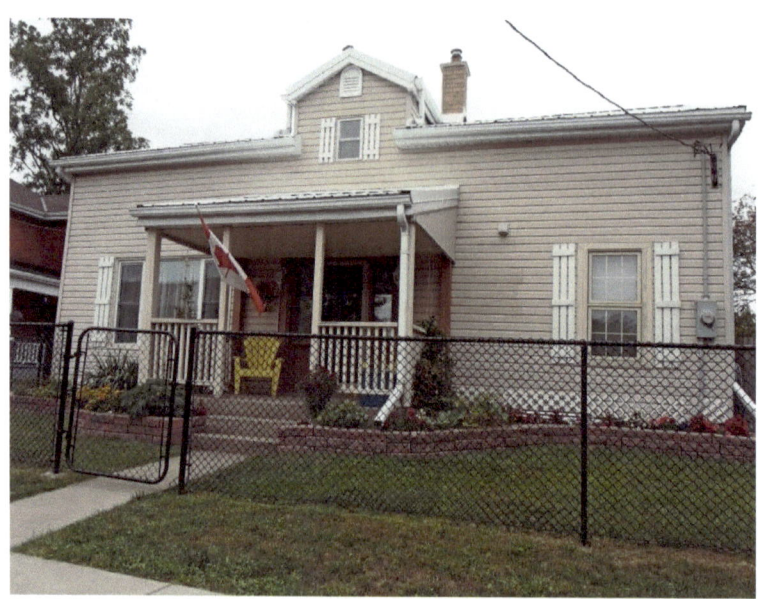

Talbot Street

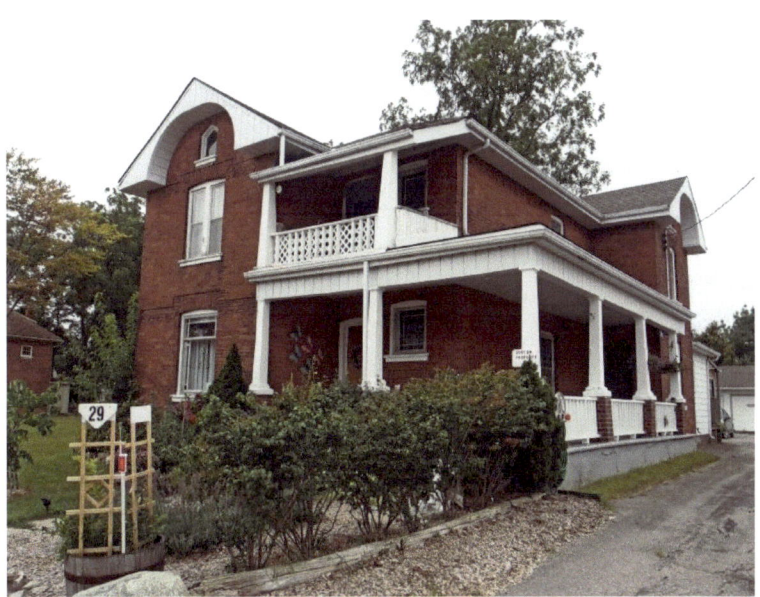

29 Talbot Street, Scotland

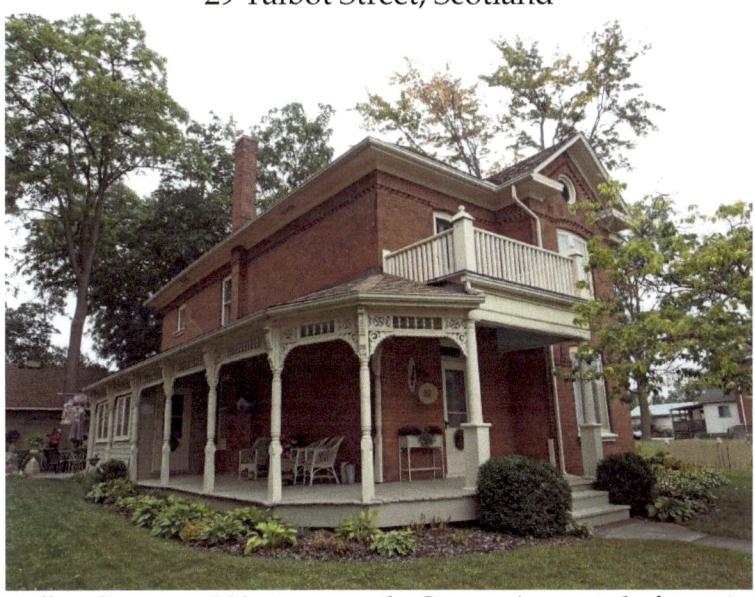

27 Talbot Street – 1890 – is an early Queen Anne style featuring a wraparound veranda with elaborate scrollwork, spool work and patterned brick work with a stringcourse at the frieze. Rusticated brick is used to ornament the principal window drip mold. Cornice return around the dormer bulls-eye window.

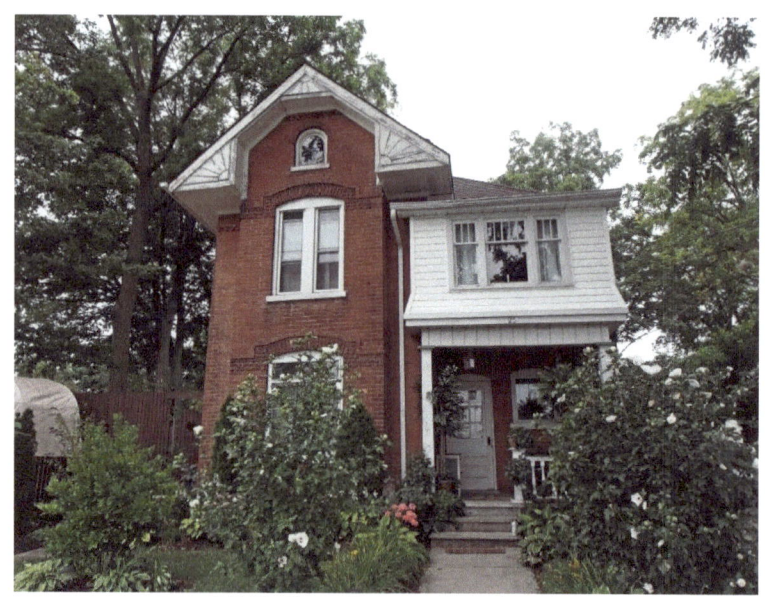

25 Talbot Street, Scotland

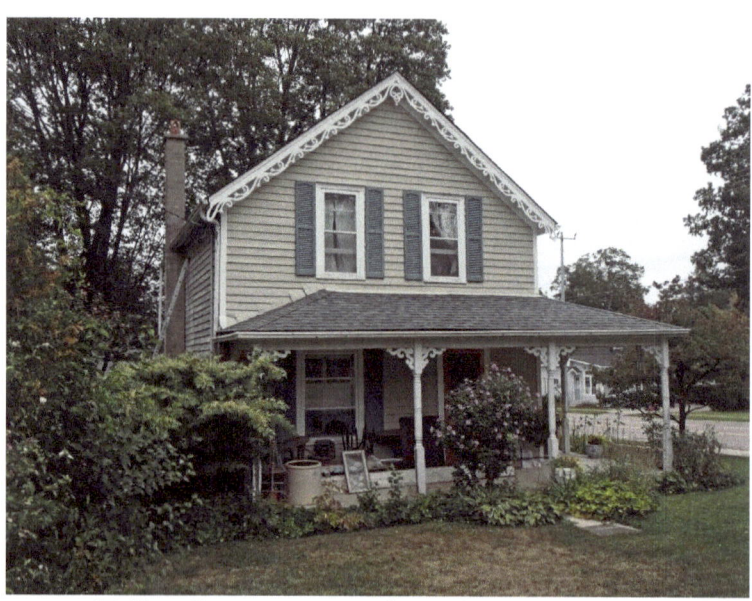

Talbot Street – verge board trim on gable

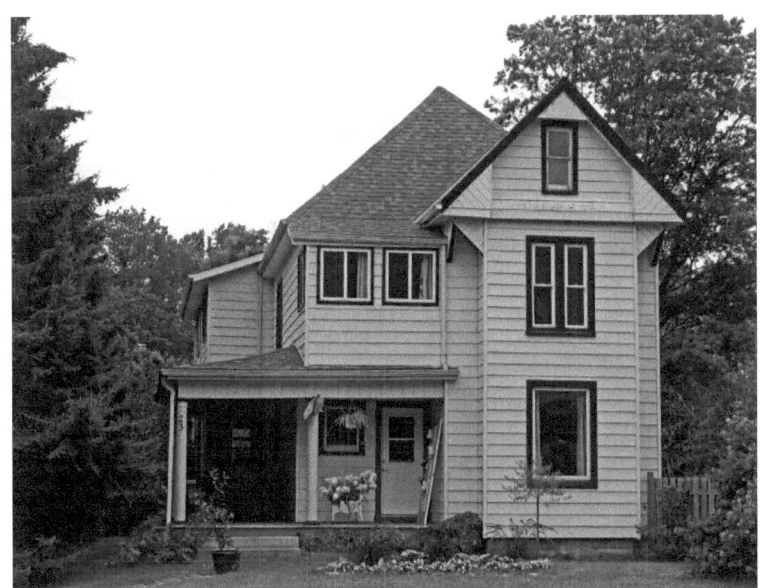

23 Talbot Street, Scotland

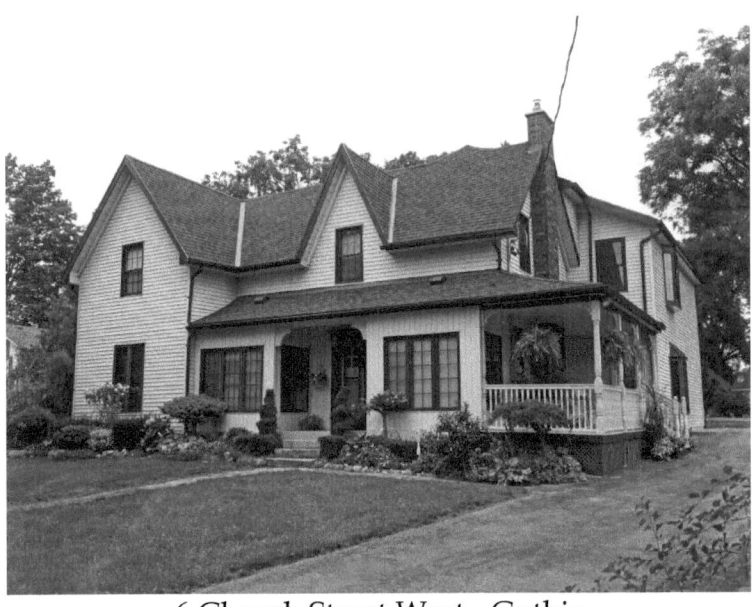

6 Church Street West - Gothic

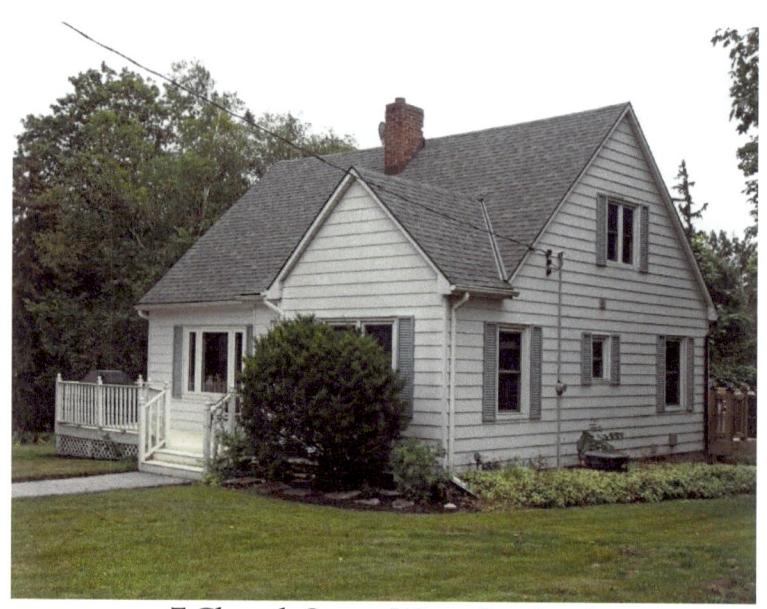

7 Church Street West, Scotland

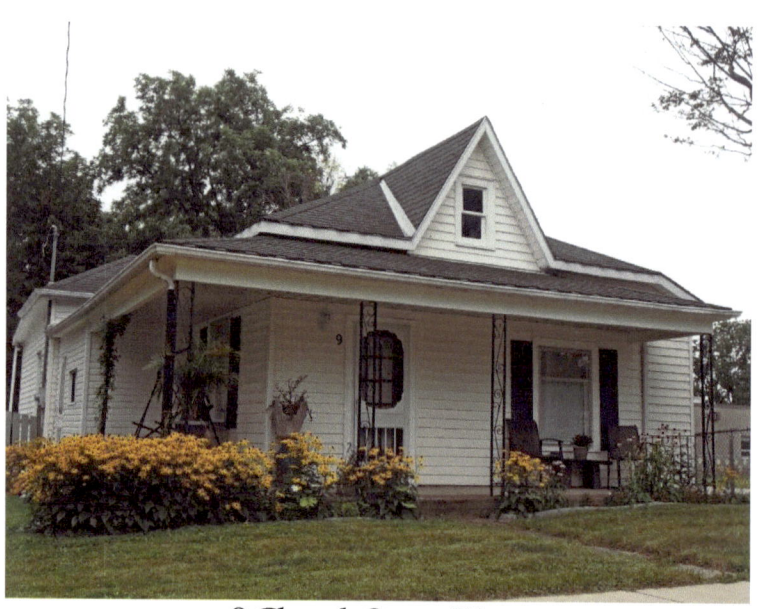

9 Church Street West

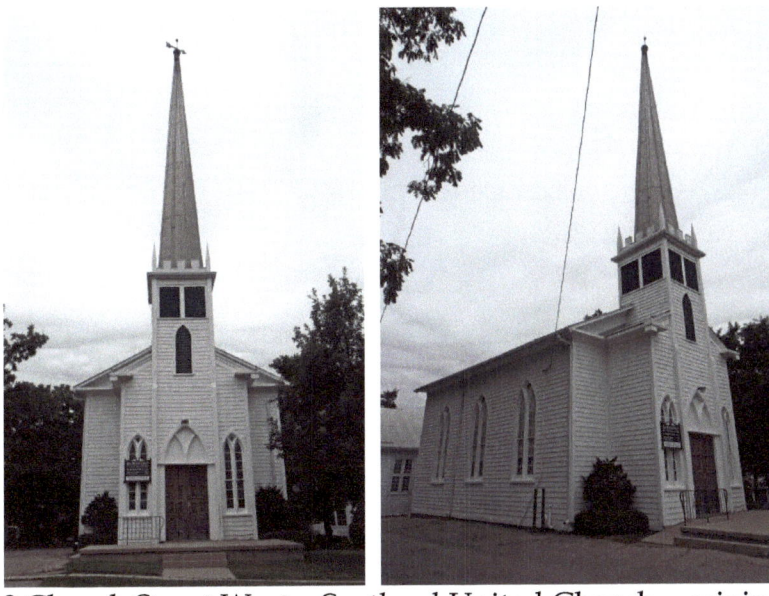

10 Church Street West – Scotland United Church – originally known as the Congregational Church – 1850 – Gothic – lancet windows, spire added in 1859

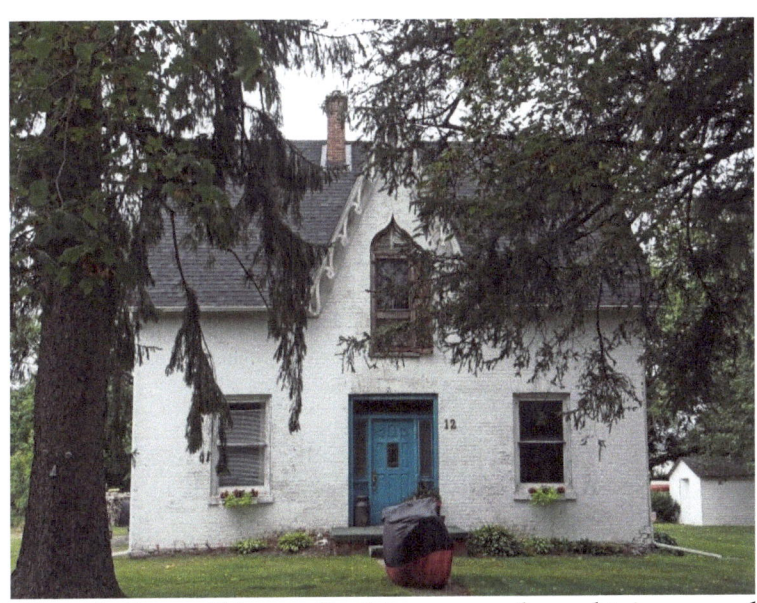

12 Church Street West – Gothic – verge board trim on gable

Architectural Terms

Bay Window: A window that projects out from a wall, in a semicircular, rectangular, or polygonal design. Used frequently in Gothic and Victorian designs. Example: 86 McLean School Road, Page 22	
Brackets: a decorative or weight-bearing structural element which forms a right angle with one side against a wall and the other under a projecting surface such as an eave or roof. Example: 125 McLean School Road, Page 21	
Buttress: a masonry structure built against or projecting from a wall which serves to support or reinforce the wall. In Canadian architecture, they are sometimes used for decoration. Example: 154 Oakland Road, Oakland, Page 46	
Cornice Return: decorative element on the end of a gable. Example: 1 Roy Street, Oakland, Page 49	
Dentil Moulding: an even series of rectangles used as ornamental decoration in cornices. Example: 74 Simcoe Street North, Page 58	
Dichromatic brickwork: the use of two colours of brick, tile or slate to decorate a façade. Example: Oakland Road, Scotland, Page 55	

Dormer: (French for "sleep") a gable end window that pierces through the plane of a sloping roof surface to create usable space in the top floor or attic of a building by adding headroom. Example: 356 St. George Road, Page 21	
Gable: the triangular portion of a wall between the edges of a sloping roof. Example: Talbot Street, Scotland, Page 62	
Hipped Roof: a roof where all sides slope downwards to the walls with no gables. Example: 356 St. George Road, Page 21	
Keystones and Voussoirs: a voussoir is a wedge-shaped element used in building an arch. A keystone is the central stone that locks all the stones into position, allowing the arch to bear weight. A keystone is often enlarged and embellished. Example: railway bridge, Page 25	
Lancet Window: a tall, narrow window with a pointed arch at its top. Example: 10 Church Street West, Scotland, Page 65	
Oriel Window - These small areas were originally set into walls and galleries for the purpose of private prayer. Over time, any projecting window or area on an upper floor was called an oriel. Example: Reid Street, Page 20	

Palladian Window: a large window that is divided into three sections with the centre section larger than the two side sections and usually arched. Example: Oakland, Page 50	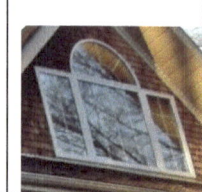
Pediment: a triangular section above the door or portico, usually supported by columns. The inside of the triangle is called the tympanum. Example: 4 King William Street, Page 15	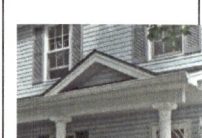
Quoin: masonry blocks at the corner of a wall, often a decorative feature, usually larger or of a different colour than the rest of the wall. Example: 7 King William Street, Page 13	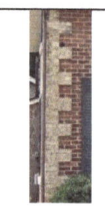
Sidelight: a vertical window that flanks a door, and is often used to emphasize the importance of a primary entrance. **Transom Window:** the light above the doorway, also called a fanlight. Example: 227 Glen Morris Road East, Page 26	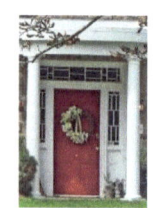
Verge board and Finial: also called bargeboards – hang from the projecting end of a roof and are often elaborately carved and ornamented. **Finial:** ornament added to the top of a gable, pinnacle, canopy or spire – a Gothic element. Example: Bethel Road, Page 35	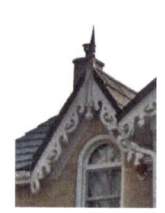

Building Styles

Classical Revival, 1820-1860 – This style was an analytical, scientific, and dogmatic revival based on intensive studies of Greek and Roman buildings, concerned with the application of Greek plans and proportions to civic buildings. Schools, libraries, government offices, and most other civic buildings were built in the Classical Revival style. The white columned porches of the Classical Revival domestic buildings are identified with the mansions of wealthy land owners in Canada. Example: 154 Bethel Road, Page 34	
Edwardian, 1900-1930 – This style bridges the ornate and elaborate styles of the Victorian era and the simplified styles of the 20th century. Edwardian Classicism provided simple, balanced facades, simple rooflines, dormer windows, large front porches, and smooth brick surfaces. Voussoirs and keystones are used sparingly and are understated. Finials and cresting are absent. Cornice brackets and braces are block-like and openings have flat arches or plain stone lintels. Example: 339 Glen Morris Road East, Page 28	
Georgian, before 1860 – This style began with the British King Georges in the 18th century. These buildings have balanced facades around a central door, medium-pitched gable roofs, and small paned windows. Example: 129 Oakland Road, Oakland, Page 48	

Gothic Revival, 1830-1890 – These decorative buildings have sharply-pitched gables with highly detailed verge boards, pointed-arch window openings, and dichromatic brickwork. It is a common style in Ontario. Example: 5 Lorimer Street, Page 7	
Italianate, 1850-1900 – A two story rectangular building with a mild hip roof, a projecting frontispiece, and generous eaves with ornate cornice brackets was the basis of the style; often there are large sash windows, quoins, ornate detailing on the windows, belvederes and wraparound verandahs. Example: 254 Glen Morris Road East, Page 27	
Neo-Gothic (Collegiate Gothic): is monochromatic and on a much grander scale than Gothic. Materials used were natural stone combined with brick. Neo-Gothic was adopted as the style for schools and universities in the early years of the 20th century. The style became so common for scholastic buildings that it is often called Collegiate Gothic. Example: 359 Regional Road 35 (Blue Lake Road), Page 30	
Ontario Cottage - one or one-and-a-half story buildings with a cottage or hip roof. The cottage roof is an equal hip roof where each hip extends to a point in the center of the roof. The hip roof has a long hip in the center. The roof can have a dormer, a belvedere, and generally two chimneys. Example: 420 Robinson Road, Bethel, Page 41	

Queen Anne, 1885-1900 – This style is distinguished by an irregular outline featuring a combination of an offset tower, broad gables, projecting two-storey bays, verandahs, multi-sloped roofs, and tall, decorative chimneys. A mixture of brick and wood is common. Windows often have one large single-paned bottom sash and small panes in the upper sash. Example: 27 Talbot Street, Page 61	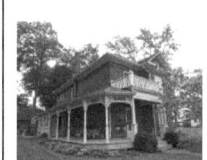
Romanesque Revival, 1880-1910 – This style hearkens back to medieval architecture of the 11th and 12th centuries with a heavy appearance, blocky towers and rounded arches. Example: 74 Simcoe Street North, Scotland, Page 59	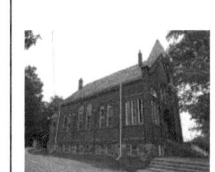
Saltbox: A saltbox is a building with a long, pitched roof that slopes down to the back, generally a wooden frame house. A saltbox has just one storey in the back and two stories in the front. The asymmetry of the unequal sides and the long, low rear roof line are the most distinctive features of a saltbox, which takes its name from its resemblance to a wooden lidded box in which salt was once kept. The earliest saltbox houses were created when a lean-to addition was added onto the rear of the original house extending the roof line sometimes to less than six feet from ground level. Example: Lorimer Street, Page 9	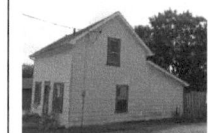

www.ingramcontent.com/pod-product-compliance
Lightning Source LLC
Chambersburg PA
CBHW040231220526
45473CB00001B/194